*Women, Religion,
and Social Change in
Brazil's Popular Church*

A TITLE FROM THE HELEN KELLOGG INSTITUTE FOR INTERNATIONAL STUDIES

GENERAL EDITOR, SCOTT MAINWARING

Women, Religion, and Social Change in Brazil's Popular Church

CAROL ANN DROGUS

UNIVERSITY OF NOTRE DAME PRESS

Notre Dame, Indiana

Designed by Jeannette Morgenroth and Wendy McMillen
Set in 10.5/14 Galliard by The Book Page, Inc.
Printed in the United States of America by Braun-Brumfield, Inc.

Library of Congress Cataloging-in-Publication Data

Drogus, Carol Ann.
    Women, religion, and social change in Brazil's popular church /
Carol Ann Drogus.
        p.   cm. — (A title from the Helen Kellogg Institute for
International Studies)
    Includes bibliographical references and index.
    ISBN 0-268-01951-7 (cloth : alk. paper)
        1. Women in the Catholic Church—Brazil—History—20th century.
    2. Basic Christian communities—Brazil.   3. Liberation theology.
    4. Brazil—Church history—20th century.   I. Title.   II. Series.
    BX1466.2.D76   1997
    282'.81'082—dc21   97-21492
                                                                    CIP

∞ *The paper used in this publication meets the minimum requirements
of the American National Standard for Information Sciences—
Permanence of Paper for Printed Library Materials, ANSI Z39.48-1984*

To two women who taught me
about faith and motherhood

Amelia Kaluger Drogus
MY MOTHER, IN LOVING MEMORY

dona Ilza
MINHA MÃE BRASILEIRA, COM CARINHO

Contents

vii

Preface

For many years, Latin Americanists considered the Catholic Church a bulwark of conservative, exclusionary political, social, and gender systems. The advent of liberation theology, however, raised the possibility that Catholicism might become a transformative cultural, social, and political force, and might even galvanize the poor to class-based political action. Accordingly, scholars increasingly asked whether and how religion might be a force for change in Latin America.

The result is a large scholarly literature on the liberationist church, some of which focuses on how liberationist ideas are interpreted in the base communities (*comunidades eclesiais de base,* or CEBs), grassroots evangelization groups of poor Catholics. A consensus now holds that interpretations in the CEBs are far from radical and far from uniform. Explaining this outcome is key to understanding the process by which elite ideas become the basis for mass action and to predicting the movement's long-term religious and social impact.

Explanations have highlighted a variety of factors, but most authors agree on the importance of individual-level variables. Many also agree on the importance of gender, recognizing women's strong presence in the CEBs. Yet gender and other individual variables have received little systematic analysis. Thus, there has been little application of relevant theory, and conclusions remain frustratingly general.

The central question this book poses is how gender affects the ways in which the religious messages of liberation theology are received and acted upon. The answer is important not only to take account of women's presence in the CEBs, but also to illuminate changing beliefs about gender and women's new organizational roles in Latin American religion and society. More broadly, the analysis also helps us to understand the powerful potential and profound limitations inherent in a religious project of social and political change.

Theoretical insights from both feminist scholarship and sociological studies of religion and politics frame the analysis of interviews with CEB members. From feminism, the book borrows the concept of a "women's culture" shaped by the public-private distinction and argues that women in the CEBs share certain characteristic tasks, roles, and attitudes that inform their response to liberation theology. Women transform the class-based message of liberation theology into terms more familiar and appealing to them, discussing their objectives in a language of charity and service to the community, particularly children. This discourse binds the women together, yet it is also compatible with a wide range of religious and political positions.

Held together by their common roles for some purposes, women nonetheless diverge significantly in their interpretations of and responses to liberation theology on the basis of their pre-existing religious orientations. Peter Benson and Dorothy Williams's analysis of religious orientation as a predictor of American political behavior proves enlightening regarding differences among Brazilian women. It reveals significant differences in the women's perceptions of God, the church, the meaning of religion, and so on, which correlate with their interpretations of the religious and political messages of liberation theology.

The Brazilian church's role in mobilizing the poor and constructing a potentially more inclusive democratic society has been more widely debated than that of any other national church, except perhaps Nicaragua. The archdiocese of São Paulo was a leader of the liberationist church. Within the archdiocese, São Miguel Paulista was known as a particularly "hot" area, providing a potentially receptive social base for a liberationist bishop and clergy who galvanized a series of social movement protests. The region thus provides an excellent "critical case."

My original data is from CEBs in the diocese of São Miguel Paulista in the eastern periphery of the city of São Paulo. It is supplemented with other, unpublished interviews conducted with women in base communities throughout the city of São Paulo by researchers from Rede Mulher, a feminist organization that works with grassroots women's movements on political, psychological, and educational issues. In addition, I utilize published studies of base communities throughout Brazil and Latin America for comparative purposes.

The data from São Miguel were gathered during a year of intensive field research in 1986, with a follow-up visit in 1990. In-depth interviews and participant-observation were the primary research techniques. As a result, the text frequently utilizes the community members' own words to paint a rich and nuanced picture of individuals living together in a social and religious community.

The results of the analysis suggest the constraints and opportunities inherent in political mobilization based on women's gender roles. They also show that religion is becoming an unexpected arena for women to rethink existing definitions of appropriate roles. Most feminist writing on this topic has been theological or prescriptive rather than sociological. Thus this book constitutes a pioneering effort in a very underresearched and undertheorized area. Yet it is also an area whose importance should not be underestimated, given religion's unquestioned importance in shaping the status of women, the fact that women are a majority of lay members and activists in religions throughout the world, and the global resurgence of religious movements for social change.

Finally, the analysis here suggests the limitations inherent in any movement to generate religious and social change. Individuals, even coreligionists, are not all religious in the same way, and so the impact of new doctrines on belief is limited. In order to mobilize people for social change, a religious movement must discover overarching themes acceptable to all. Gender unexpectedly emerges as a stronger force than class to bind poor, urban women together for social action. The constraints inherent in women's culturally (and religiously) defined gender roles, however, ultimately limit mobilization and change.

My first and deepest debt is owed to the women in the CEBs in Santo Antônio, who received me into their meetings, worship services, and homes as a friend. Dona Ilza, who appears here under a pseudonym, became my adoptive Brazilian mother and an important influence on my life. I was extremely fortunate to come to know all these women, and sharing their daily lives in some small degree has given me a much deeper appreciation of "Brazilian reality" than anything else could.

Thanks are also due to the numerous individuals who generously gave of their time and talents to read and comment on many parts and versions of these chapters, especially Daniel Levine, Scott Mainwaring, Booth Fowler, Hannah Stewart-Gambino, Edward Cleary, John Burdick, Madeleine Adriance Cousineau, Roderic Camp, and Ted Hewitt. Special thanks to Daniel Levine and Scott Mainwaring for support that enabled me to spend a year at the Helen Kellogg Institute for International Studies at the University of Notre Dame working on this manuscript and related projects. The Kellogg Institute provided me with an excellent support staff and access to many references not available at a small college in upstate New York, as well as time to write, and an intellectually stimulating environment.

Finally, I could not have completed the field work for this book or its writing without the constant support and encouragement of my husband, Steve Orvis. Thanks also to my sons, Nick and Will, for their patience and their love. My understanding of the significance of family relationships for the women in Santo Antônio owes much to the meaning these three have given to my own life.

ONE

Popular Church, Women's Church

Listening to Women in Brazil's Base Communities

In 1987, women from Christian base communities in the Catholic parish of Santo Antônio in São Paulo's poor eastern periphery celebrated International Women's Day. To commemorate the event, they designed a poster bearing the slogan "Women! Make History!" emblazoned above a lithograph depicting a woman with upraised arm, bursting the confines of a house. The slogan was more than mere rhetoric: since 1980, Santo Antônio, like many poor urban areas throughout Latin America, had been galvanized by a series of social movements challenging the government to improve living conditions. Contrary to the expectations of both social science and popular wisdom, poor, religious women from the base communities were in the forefront of this activism in Brazil and throughout the region.

Women's mobilization and politicization were unexpected consequences of the creation of the Popular Church, a movement identified spiritually with liberation theology, and organizationally with the Christian base communities. As one author observed of El Salvador, "The surprise in the birthing of the *Iglesia Popular* (Popular Church) is that the midwives are women" (Golden 1991, 38). Liberation theology set out to shake the Catholic Church out of centuries of passive and active support for the existing social order. It envisioned religion as a source of cultural, political, and social change. That change was to come through a process of consciousness-raising in the base communities—small grassroots communities of the poor—that would lead the poor to recognize and act upon their oppression as a social class.

The liberationist message, with its emphasis on exploitation of the poor as workers, was most clearly directed at the situation of poor men. When priests and nuns carried the consciousness-raising techniques, radical symbolism, and class analysis to poor urban areas, however, women were more likely than their husbands to respond to the call to form base communities (*comunidades eclesiais de base,* or CEBs). One nun working in a factory and living in a poor urban community noted: "The CEBs don't have an adequate structure for workers. The factory influences them for forty-eight hours, the CEB for two. I perceived then that the church did not reach youth or workers, but only women, old people, and children, whose life is centered in the neighborhood. . . . In the CEBs, the majority are women" (Nunes 1985, 178).[1] Base communities are not exclusively female preserves, of course. In Brazil as a whole, women represented about 55 to 60 percent of all members in 1994 (Pierucci and Prandi 1995, 22, 29). In many urban communities especially, however, the day-to-day audience—the core workers who organize the masses, catechism classes, novenas, and often the social movements as well—is female. Cecilia Mariz's informal survey of sixteen CEBs in Pernambuco found that 74 percent of the leaders were women (Mariz 1989, 84). In urban São Paulo, two-thirds to 90 percent of base community members are women (Hewitt 1985, 120; "Aos animadores").

This book explores the significance of this fact for women, for the Catholic Church, and for society. It asks whether religious experience is gendered and, if so, what impact this has had on the liberationist project of religious and political change. To answer the second question is to ask as well what the liberationist experience has meant for women. What effect did participation in the base communities have on their religious beliefs, political attitudes, and behavior? Finally, this book asks how the experience of the base communities may have changed women's thinking about themselves and their roles in the family, the church, and society.

RELIGION, CULTURE, AND POLITICS

Only twenty-five years ago, it would have seemed strange to ask what role religion, particularly Catholicism, might play in political and social change in Latin America. The problematic linkage was not between religion and politics or society. On the contrary, many scholars saw Latin American politics and culture as profoundly shaped by a Catholic ethos. Precisely because Catholicism appeared to be the source of deeply ingrained political and cultural beliefs, social scientists of many stripes—Marxists, functionalists, feminists—deemed it incapable of generating change, and especially "progressive" change.

Catholicism arguably stood as an obstacle to social change in the direction of greater equality and democracy in two areas especially, political culture and gender relations. Scholarship generally pointed to three means by which the church buttressed inegalitarian relationships. First, institutional structures and politics tied the church to elite groups, whether political or gender elites. Second, the larger religious ethos of official Catholicism—doctrine, ritual, beliefs—seemed to be a powerful conservative cultural force. Third, popular religion, though quite different from the official religion, also seemed a substantial obstacle to progressive change.

In the realm of politics and political culture, much research focused on the link between the institutional church and the state.[2] From that perspective, the church seemed firmly linked to the interests of conservative elites. It repeatedly sided with and gave legitimacy to authoritarian regimes throughout the region, often in exchange for recognition of church privileges. The second source of church influence, official doctrine and symbolism, also seemed to shape the region's "two-class, authoritarian, traditional, elitist, patrimonial, Catholic, stratified, hierarchical, and corporate" political culture (Wiarda 1973, 209). Religious reinforcement of this authoritarian political culture originated in Iberian Catholicism's corporatist, feudal, and antidemocratic tendencies (Wiarda 1973). Popular religious practices seemed to further buttress political practices such as patron-clientelism, with its hierarchical structures, dependence of the masses on elite benefactors, and impediments to effecting intraclass political mobilization. Moreover, the otherworldly quality of folk Catholicism arguably led poor individuals to channel their efforts toward propitiating the supernatural elements, rather than organizing collective political action for change (de Kadt 1967).

Feminist scholars modified mainstream sociological theories of religion and applied these to the analysis of gender relations. They concluded that religion was "the major cultural reinforcer of modern industrial patriarchy" (Briggs 1987, 408). In Latin America, feminists saw Mediterranean Catholicism reinforcing a conservative gender ideology in much the same way it reinforced an unequal and exclusionary political culture. The institutional church's actions, such as opposition to divorce and birth control, contributed to women's subordination. So, too, did official Catholic doctrine which stressed women's domesticity and proper vocation as wife and mother. In its popular folk version, *marianismo*, Catholicism's exaltation of the Virgin Mary simultaneously raised women to a level of moral superiority and excluded them from participation in the public realm. Indeed, the term *marianismo* came to describe not only a complex web of beliefs and devotional practices centered on Mary, but also a social norm, the inverse of *machismo*, that perpetuates women's subordination, especially in the public realm.[3]

Static theories of religion's conservative political and social impact, however, ignore the fact that religion has always been a crucial element in stimulating political action by the Latin American poor, including women. A team of Mexican researchers claim that "For the Latin American people, the leaders in whom they have confidence are religious leaders. . . . Movements of popular rebellion have been religious movements although not always inspired by priests. But a popular movement always needs religious motives. . . ."[4] Such theories also ignore the multifaceted nature of religious belief, concluding that religiously inspired popular movements must be reactionary, "traditionalizing," or in some way "pre-political."[5] But while *some* religiously motivated movements may have these characteristics, religion is not always and inevitably a conservative force with respect to either politics or patriarchy.

In different contexts, David Laitin (Africa) and Daniel Levine (Latin America) have stressed the mutability and complexity of religious symbols. Laitin points out that multiple strands in religious traditions make them particularly open to reinterpretation:

> any religion encompasses a number of traditions that are in some degree in conflict. . . . World religions constitute complex social realities; and adherents to those religions are not limited in their repertoires for action by a single system of symbols. Religious adherents have available to them the original books and founding ideology, the various traditions of the priests, and the contemporary development of the religion elsewhere in the world. (Laitin 1986, 24)

Levine notes that such complexity can provide a basis for change in even the most "conservative" religion: "it is not religion per se which produces conservative effects, but rather a particular set of historically determined concepts, tradition, and organizational commitments. As these change, we may expect new models of social and political action to arise in association with them" (Levine 1980, 16).

The multifaceted nature of religious symbols opens them to conflicting interpretations, some with conservative and others with quite radical implications for social, political, and cultural change. This fact was brought home to students of Latin American religion and politics by the advent of liberation theology and the growth of the Popular Church.[6] The church's public commitment to a preferential option for the poor at the regional bishops' conference in Medellín (1968) meant that Catholicism in Latin America could no longer be looked at as a static, conservative force in politics. Since that time, most scholars have come to take "change in religion . . . as normal and continuous," and have also stressed the primacy and autonomy of religious motivations for political action and social change (Levine 1991, 683).[7]

At about the same time, feminists also began to reassess their conclusion that religion inevitably contributed to women's subordination. The women's spirituality movement and feminist theologies of liberation suggested that reworked religious ideas could be a source of empowerment rather than subordination for women. Consensus on religion's mutability and potentially liberating role is considerably less widespread among feminists than among mainstream students of religion and politics, however, and most feminist theory still casts doubt on the ability of a movement initiated in a male-dominated church to emancipate women.

The central issue for Latin American religion in any case was what impact liberation theology's new ideas would have on society and politics. Liberation theologians only gradually modified their class analysis to include other forms of subordi-

nation, such as sexism and racism. Moreover, most early feminist theology was written in the United States and Europe,
emerging in Latin America only in the early 1980s. In addition, the male-dominated structure of the church itself, as well
as the assumption that the main audience for liberation theology was defined by class ("the poor") helped to sharpen the
scholarly focus on liberation theology's likely effect on political rather than gender-related change.

As a result, very little attention has been paid to women's
role in the Popular Church, despite the fact that historically
and culturally women were considered the primary bearers
of religion in Latin America.[8] As Daniel Levine points out,
"There has . . . been scant attention to issues of gender, such
as the roles women occupy in religious symbols and structures, or the specific way in which gender affects the reception of religious or social messages" (Levine 1991, 685). Yet it
seems increasingly clear that "gender turns out to be a major
determinant of how messages are received and what is viewed
as legitimate action" (Levine 1991, 688). Moreover, it is also
plausible that women's new status, roles, and activities in the
base communities contribute to changing gender attitudes and
relations. It is time to reassess the Popular Church as a wom-
en's church, asking both how women's experiences and perceptions have shaped the radical project of the liberationist
church and how participation in that project has affected
women's lives. Such an assessment is necessary to understand
fully religion's potential as a force for political and cultural
change in Latin America.

GENDER: MEDIATING CHANGE, CHANGING RELATIONS?

In recent years women's numerical predominance in the CEBs
has received increasing recognition, so that it is now common
to find references to the CEBs as primarily women's organiza-

tions, or to have note taken of women's day-to-day responsibility for carrying on the work of the Popular Church. At the
same time, feminist scholars have increasingly noted the origins of many urban working-class women's movements in the
Popular Church. The church is, according to some feminist
scholars, one of several major strands that fed the growth of a
regional women's movement during and prior to redemocrati-
zation (Jaquette 1991, 6). Yet despite this growing recognition, analysis of women in the Popular Church remains rare.[9]

The empirical fact of women's predominance and the relative neglect of women's roles point to a serious gap in our
understanding of the Popular Church. They would alone not
be enough to justify a focus on gender issues. There are, however, also compelling theoretical reasons for looking at women
in the Popular Church.

Gender as a Filter for Religious Experience

Liberation theology's impact is likely to occur through gradual, diffuse changes in culture, rather than through a dramatic
impact on political behavior. Although it may have real long-
term social implications, such diffuse change can be difficult
to perceive (Levine 1992; Escobar 1992). Assessing it requires
looking at the way liberationist ideas are taken up, reconcep-
tualized, and used to generate both political behavior and
new cultural attitudes in the Christian base communities.[10] In
other words, we must understand the process by which ordi-
nary believers interpret their faith and the world in the CEBs.
As noted above, there is a growing consensus that gender may
be one important factor in this process of interpretation. Thus,
analysis of gender as a factor is a prerequisite to answering
larger questions about liberation theology. Theoretically, however, it is also a legitimate area for inquiry in its own right.

The empirical fact of women's predominance in the CEBs
suggests some theoretical reasons for positing gender's impor-

tance. Throughout Latin America, women bear the burden of advancing Catholic movements—whether conservative or radical—and carrying on the religious life of communities on a day-to-day basis.[11] Women in the base communities in Santo Antônio remembered, "When we began to get together, there were just the women." And one Salvadoran base community, reflecting on its evolution, noted, "The chapel was a place for women" (Golden 1991, 41). Women throughout the region have a quantitatively distinct relationship to religion, participating in ritual and sacraments more, praying more, and organizing more than men.[12]

Women's quantitatively greater religious activity suggests one important sense in which religiosity is "gendered": in Latin America, and indeed it seems throughout the Mediterranean Catholic world, religion falls into women's sphere of interests and competence despite their lack of formal authority in the church. Women are expected to be more religious and to maintain religious teachings, morals, and traditions in the home and community (Stevens 1973). The sexual division of religious labor may have implications for the way women perceive the church, religious symbolism, tradition, innovation, and so on, as well as for their higher levels of participation.

The broader cultural division of labor into a private, female sphere and a public, male one may also have an impact on women's religious experience. This possibility is glimpsed in descriptions of women as not only more actively religious but also more emotionally involved and seeking particular kinds of solace from religion:

> We came together, men and women, but the women had many more troubles and pains to talk to God about. The misery is the same for everyone, but women live with it day and night, seeing the children cry from hunger, watching their stomachs swollen with worms. To them falls the care

of the children with diseases that can't be cured, to them falls seeing the children die without being able to do anything. The women are the ones who know everyday that there is not enough, that there are only tortillas and salt. . . . She feels more deeply all the bad things and even ends up feeling guilty about them. . . . Sunday, in the chapel, everything could be forgotten. (Golden 1991, 41)

Here, members of a Salvadoran base community posit religion as "gendered" not only in terms of quantity but also in terms of the quality of the religious experience.[13] The source of differential religious experiences, they suggest, lies in the different roles men and women fulfill in a gender-based division of labor.[14] Women's socialization and their distinctive responsibilities as caregivers for the physical and psychological well-being of children, in particular, may color their religious and other life experiences in fundamental ways.

A variant on this approach stresses divergence in men's and women's psychological and moral development, whether or not these originate in a gender-based division of labor. It has become common in feminist studies, for example, to posit a "women's voice." Such a voice may or may not reflect the psychological requirements of women's gender-assigned roles. Many studies leave aside that issue altogether. In any case, certain behaviors and attitudes are described as characteristically female and as characteristic of a female interpretation and understanding of issues. Women, for example, are held to emphasize interconnectedness and interpersonal relations more than men (Gilligan 1982). They may also have a distinctive set of values stressing the preservation of life and the development of socially acceptable behavior (Ruddick 1980). They may communicate in a distinctive way that demonstrates a commitment to interpersonal interconnectedness rather than hierarchy (Tannen 1990).

Religion has not been exempt from attempts to show that interpretations from a "women's perspective" might produce substantially different readings of accepted symbols and values. Some of this literature has reflected a feminist view, described earlier, that male-dominated religions centered on a male God reinforce women's subordination because they perpetuate dependence on males and a sense of the illegitimacy of female authority (Christ 1982; Schneiders 1983). In other cases, however, authors have simply sought to demonstrate that fundamental religious concepts such as sin and salvation may be interpreted quite differently by women and men (Saiving 1979).

Generally speaking this literature has remained theoretical or prescriptive rather than empirical. That is, women theologians or others have asked how a particular "male-defined" religious concept might look from women's perspective and provided an answer based on logical extrapolation from their perception of women's distinctive worldview. Such studies have rarely had recourse to surveys or interviews to ascertain whether women do, indeed, generally hold a particular, gender-identified view.

There is, however, at least some sociological evidence to support the claim that men and women interpret religious symbols differently. One study found, for example, that "girls were more likely to depict God as loving, comforting and forgiving, while boys tended to view God as a supreme power, forceful planner and controller" (Batson and Ventis 1982, 4). This difference in perception of God actually fits rather neatly with many feminist descriptions of women's "different voice." Similarly, there is some evidence to indicate that one fundamental divide in types of religiosity involves the extent to which people experience religion as an individual relationship with God (agentic) or a relationship with God through others (communal).[15] Although it is unclear whether these categories cut across genders or capture some male-female differences, the two types initially sprang from research which identified them as typically male (agentic) and female (communal) (Bakan 1966).

In sum, several hypotheses suggest that gender mediates religious experience, adding weight to existing studies that suggest the importance of "developing an understanding of the way gender shapes the experience of being and becoming a religious person" (Davidman and Greil 1994, 109). First, women's assignment of a particular role in a religious division of labor may influence the quantity and quality of their participation. Second, public-private distinctions and corresponding divisions of male-female roles and responsibilities may shape women's needs, interests, and perceptions in ways that influence their religious lives. Third, and more simply, women's different psychological and moral development, whatever its source, may lead them to interpret many issues and topics, including religious symbols, differently than a "male-defined" norm.

If women experience religion and religious symbolism differently than men, this could have important consequences for a project of religious-cultural change such as the Popular Church. It could lead women to interpret the new, liberationist religious symbolism in distinctive and unexpected ways. Indeed, this possibility might be particularly strong in the case of liberation theology, when a doctrine developed almost exclusively by men is propagated in communities composed of a majority of women.

The question of what happens in the CEBs when doctrine becomes lived faith, then, can be restated much more specifically: What happens to the doctrine of intellectual male clerics when it becomes the lived faith of working-class lay women? Asking this question is essential to understanding the probable effect of liberation theology on culture and politics, as it leads us to clarify how women's attitudes and political behavior are changed by their experiences in the CEBs. It may also lead us to ask whether this experience changes women's perceptions of themselves, their roles, and male-female relations—whether women's religious and political experiences in the CEBs may not contribute to changing patriarchal as well as political and cultural values.

Religion as a Shaper of Gender Relations

There is little doubt that religion is important in defining gender role attitudes and behavior. A variety of studies, particularly in the United States and other industrialized countries, have demonstrated that even in arguably more secularized countries, religion continues to play a key role in defining appropriate gender roles and relations.[16] The fact that religion is most often identified with the private sphere may be particularly salient in legitimizing gender roles for women, since they are also culturally identified with that sphere.

Feminist writers have advanced a number of theories about the ways in which religion, particularly Christian religion, may maintain unequal, traditional gender roles and relations. Religious language that uses the "universal male" form, religious symbols that reflect ambivalence about women, male dominance in hierarchically organized religious institutions, and even the focus on a male God may exclude and delegitimize women as authorities.[17] In addition, religious teaching often directly addresses the appropriate model of family life and in doing so has typically stressed a family division of labor in which women are identified with the private sphere.

This list is not exhaustive, but it demonstrates that feminist scholars have found numerous reasons to believe that religion reinforces traditional role expectations and women's subordination. Yet a closer examination of the list suggests that religions may differ greatly with respect to these features, so that some may offer greater opportunities for women to reassess traditional roles and empower themselves than others. Indeed, cross-denominational research carried out in North America indicates that Christian religious groups vary considerably in the extent to which they reinforce traditional gender role models (Porter and Albert 1977; Brinkerhoff and Mackie 1984 and 1985; Heaton and Cornwall 1989). Moreover, a static model of religion as a source of gender-role traditionalism ignores religions' evolution. Religious institutions, like others, accommodate and sometimes encourage changing social trends, including changing gender roles (Thornton 1985).

Finally, as others have noted with respect to religion's political impact, religious traditions and symbolism are rich, complex, and multifaceted. Their very complexity may facilitate women's use of religious symbols and concepts for personal and political empowerment, even within male-dominated churches. Feminist spirituality is only one possible religious route to personal empowerment for women. Women take advantage of the complexities and contradictory messages in even quite conservative religions to map out and legitimize new and empowering dimensions for their lives. Women "returning" to orthodox Judaism, for example, may utilize its rigid constructions of gender roles in ways that empower them rather than reaffirm patriarchal values and practices (Kaufman 1985). Similarly, American women Pentecostal preachers exploit the "tension between the God-given inferiority of women submissive to men and the belief in equality before God" to pursue nontraditional roles (Lawless 1988b, 145–46). Latin American Pentecostal women also seem to follow such a path (Brusco 1986).

Reform Catholicism, as embodied in liberation theology, cannot simply be dismissed as a bearer of patriarchy. In order to assess a religion's potential for empowering women, we must seek to understand the messages and opportunities it provides for them, and the space it may provide for women to develop their own critiques and variations on religious themes. Returning to the feminist critiques of religion outlined above, we can see that there are two broad mechanisms through which religion is thought to shape gender roles: ideas and organizational structures.

We need to look at each of these areas systematically in order to see what possibilities the Popular Church offers for women's empowerment. Specifically, we need to ask about ideas: what messages does religious symbolism convey about gender roles? What are the religion's overt teachings concerning gender and family? In regard to structures: what roles and opportunities are available for women within the religious organization? What kinds of extrareligious roles does the religion encourage women to take on? Are these in the private or public sphere? Answering these questions with respect to the Popular Church produces a portrait of mixed messages, but it is also one that opens at least some possibilities for women to redefine their gender roles.

Women in Christian Base Communities: The Debate

There are, then, theoretical as well as empirical reasons to analyze the interaction of religion and gender in the base communities. As the foregoing discussion suggests, that analysis may usefully be approached from two directions. First, what role does gender play in the interpretation of religious ideas and activism in the CEBs? Second, how, if at all, have the base communities contributed to the development of gender consciousness and the empowerment of women?

The two questions are related in a variety of ways. For example, gender may affect women's mobilization in CEB-sponsored political and social movements; at the same time, participation in such public-sphere activities may have an impact on women's roles and self-image. It is also important to pay attention to the possibility of differences in women's religiosity and to ask how the nature of their religious lives and beliefs may be reflected in their attitudes toward gender relations. For these deeply religious women, it would be a mistake to assess a degree of "gender consciousness" in a vacuum, just as it is a mistake to make assumptions about CEB members' political consciousness without considering their religious beliefs. Daniel Levine's admonition to "take religion seriously" and "work outward from religious beliefs" applies as much to the assessment of gender attitudes as to the assessment of political beliefs.

These two questions—how gender mediates religious belief and how religion influences attitudes about gender roles—have usually been treated separately. In part this may reflect a division of labor between scholars of religion, who focus on the first, and feminist scholars, who tend to focus on the second. In practice this division is not nearly so neat, but it may be useful to separate the two questions here in order to describe the range of conclusions advanced so far.

Extremely little research has focused on the questions of whether and how gender might play a mediating role in the base communities. Yet these questions are crucial not only to understanding women's experiences per se, but also to developing an interpretation of the Popular Church's political and social impact. Thus far, two schools of thought have emerged in the literature. One suggests that women's high level of participation in the base communities constitutes evidence of religious traditionalism. Women are historically the main constituency for religious groups of all types and have especially been the target of movements to reassert traditional religious values. Because they are the bearers of religious tradition, women's higher level of participation may itself indicate religious traditionalism, if women are more likely to bring traditional, conservative religious values to the Popular Church.[18] From this perspective, gender is a mediating variable and one with specific consequences: it deradicalizes and traditionalizes the Popular Church.

Other scholars have also hypothesized that gender acts as a filter for liberationist messages, but as Daniel Levine points out, we have little evidence of just what this filtering process consists of (Levine 1991). Some studies have suggested specific ways in which women reinterpret liberation theology, usually noting that they do so in ways that make its political content more compatible with presumed female values such as cooperation, community, and nurturance of children (Drogus 1990; Levine 1992; Burdick 1992).

Much more attention has been paid to the question of how participation in the base communities affects women's gender consciousness. Three major positions have emerged. Some writers, including many liberation theologians, portray the base communities as a unique experience offering empowerment to poor women. They stress the opportunities for leadership and the egalitarian atmosphere that the communities offer women (see Hewitt 1991, 63; Goldsmit and Sweeney 1988). Similarly, Daniel Levine points out that the groups certainly offer opportunities to otherwise marginalized women, and that these may lead to changes in their self-image and family lives (Levine 1992). Renny Golden concludes from research in El Salvador that faith motivates and empowers women, although she is not specific about the attributes of the base communities that contribute to this process (Golden 1991).

In contrast, although feminist scholar Sonia Alvarez recognizes that the church played a role in the evolution of the women's movement by gathering women together for political action, she contends that the church has stymied their development of gender consciousness. She admits that the church may have empowered women as citizens. She argues, however, that church doctrine, symbols, and practices remain sexist, and that the church has openly hindered women's discussion of feminist issues and has excluded women from leadership roles (Alvarez 1990, 1991).[19]

Finally, W. E. Hewitt stakes out a midrange position. He argues that the CEBs do provide substantial opportunities for women to develop leadership skills, new roles, and a nascent gender consciousness. While the Popular Church has not contributed directly to the empowerment of women and opportunities are limited, he finds that many women are able to overcome obstacles and use their experience in the CEBs to take on new roles. He concludes that women's opportunities are limited, but more substantial "than many feminist observers would admit" (Hewitt 1991, 66).

Thus, we have at least some propositions to consider with respect to both the gendered nature of religious belief in the Popular Church, and the church's impact on gender attitudes. The research to date, however, has generally not been informed by the specific theoretical considerations outlined above. Moreover, the conclusions reached have often been rather reductionist in nature, in treating certain attitudes as typically "female," rather than exploring possible differences among women. Finally, commentaries have generally focused on the implications of the liberationist church for women's liberation and have only rarely linked conclusions about the degree of women's gender consciousness with insights about their religious beliefs and political convictions. Yet base communities, despite the predominance of women, are not gender-consciousness movements. They are religious organizations with political implications. It is impossible to draw valid conclusions about their members' experiences and attitudes unless we appreciate fully the religious dimensions of their lives.

WOMEN, RELIGION, AND SOCIAL CHANGE:
UNDERSTANDING THE CONNECTIONS

This book explores the connections among gender, religion, and social change by asking both how gender influences women's interpretations of liberation theology and how their experiences in the Popular Church affect women's attitudes toward gender roles. It attempts to avoid classifying the women's political and gender attitudes in predetermined social science categories and instead tries to highlight how their views of politics, community, family, and self emerge from their religious beliefs. While the research was conducted in Brazil, wherever possible I incorporate insights from studies throughout Latin America.

Analyzing a single case seemed a particularly appropriate way to study the 'participants' subjective perspectives, and the complex interaction that leads to political behavior. Rather than quantifying how many members agreed with certain liberationist language or participated in specific political activities, I wished to explore the different meanings participants attached to religious and political concepts and activities. In order to understand how gender, religion, class, and other variables came together to shape a CEB member's view of politics or gender relations, I relied on both in-depth interviews and extended participant observation in seven CEBs in Santo Antônio. A total of fifty-four individuals, including pastoral workers, were interviewed, although the core sample of lay women comprised thirty interviewees. In addition to the interviews, I noted interactions and statements made by the interviewees at CEB meetings, religious observances, parties, political meetings, and other events over the course of a year (1986). As often as possible, I utilize the women's own words in interviews and community events to illustrate their views.

The choice of Santo Antônio as a research site was based on two factors: its approximation to a "critical case," and access to the CEBs. In choosing a critical case, I followed the *a fortiori* principle that if liberation theology does not flourish in the conditions its proponents have deemed most hospitable, it is unlikely to do so elsewhere. Santo Antônio presents an especially propitious context for the CEBs: the kind of area of poor and working-class people that liberationists describe as fertile ground, it is located in an archdiocese and diocese that, at the time of the research, were committed to the Popular Church. Santo Antônio is located in the extreme northeastern periphery of São Paulo, not quite thirty kilometers from the city's central plaza, Praça da Sé. It is one of the city's poorest regions. Only about 20 percent of homes there are connected to sanitation, and though most have electricity, only 5 percent have telephones. Nearly two-thirds of families subsist on five minimum salaries or less, compared with 48 percent nationwide, and 18.4 percent in the wealthiest areas of São Paulo (Caldeira 1984, 27-28).[20]

Itaim Paulista, the electoral district in which the parish is located, is politically typical of poor regions of the city. In 1982, 17.3 percent of the population voted for the leftist *Partido dos Trabalhadores* (PT, or Workers' Party), compared with 18.5 percent of socioeconomically similar areas, and 14.9 percent of the city as a whole. In 1985, Itaim Paulista distributed its vote almost exactly according to the average for similar regions, giving 25.7 percent to the PT. In the city as a whole, it received 20.7 percent. Thus, the region voted to the left of the city as a whole, but close to the norm for poor, peripheral areas (Lamounier 1986, pp. 112 and 95).

In contrast to other poor areas, however, Itaim Paulista and the diocese encompassing it, São Miguel Paulista, were also known for political activism and social movements in the

1980s—and for having a strongly liberationist church that stimulated these activities (Hewitt 1985; Caldeira 1984). Particularly during the formative years of the base communities, the region was led by a famously liberationist bishop, dom Angêlico Sândalo Bernardino, and pastoral workers with a clear liberationist agenda. As a result, it experienced early and unusually rapid CEB formation (Hewitt 1985). Thus, the socioeconomic characteristics that many would expect to predispose the area to a liberationist agenda were reinforced by the pastoral orientation of the region, making it a strong candidate for a "critical case."

Within this "critical case" region, however, I was dependent upon contacts with pastoral agents to locate an appropriate parish, particularly since CEBs do not exist in every parish and generally do not have recorded addresses. Moreover, speaking to many very skeptical pastoral workers convinced me that I would not be well received if I walked into a community on my own. I interviewed many pastoral agents, particularly nuns, throughout the city, and they directed me to friends in other areas. I also attended religious retreats and conferences in order to meet pastoral workers.

Ultimately, I met a pastoral worker in the archdiocesan headquarters who resides in Santo Antônio. She invited me to attend a retreat for CEB members sponsored by the parish. As a participant in the retreat, I met several other pastoral workers in the region and had direct contact with many CEB members. The lay members were much more receptive to my presence than the pastoral agents, and I left the retreat with contacts in a number of CEBs.

Through these activists, I quickly gained access to others. References from friends in other communities proved sufficient to produce an invitation to a meeting, and introductions to people present. As I became known among the leaders, I was able to hear of and attend a variety of meetings, retreats, novenas, and so on. At these events I was often able to extend my contacts further.

Having created a network of potential respondents, my data collection took two forms: interviews with thirty women, and participant observation. In selecting women to interview, I tried to include a cross section of regularly attending members, from less active women to the leadership. Regular attendance was important to ensure that respondents had in fact had ample opportunity to be exposed to liberationist ideas.[21] Interviewing leaders was relatively easy: many had described their experiences in the CEB in other contexts, and they were quite willing to recount them to me. They were, however, reluctant to help me arrange to interview privately those women they considered "less informed." Moreover, the "less informed" themselves were often somewhat reticent about expressing their views, directing me instead to people they thought would "know more." This difficulty was eventually overcome by sheer persistence in attending meetings and getting to know a variety of members.

In many cases, I interviewed the same women on several occasions. At times, for example, I did initial interviews with the "less conscious" women in mixed groups, and then requested an individual follow-up interview. I interviewed women either at the church or, more frequently, in their homes. Interview sessions lasted from about an hour and a half to as much as four hours. I began interviews with demographic and other "informational" questions, proceeding to potentially more controversial questions. To facilitate uninhibited responses, I often allowed the flow of conversation to dictate the order in which questions were asked. One topic frequently led to another according to the interests and concerns of the respondent. The fact that I was a foreigner also enabled me to ask "ignorant" questions. This meant that respondents could explain certain CEB symbols or practices to me in their own terms, without fearing that I already had an idea of what the "right" answer was. Many women were also anxious to explain their views to me so that I could "communicate" them to people in America. Once the actual interviews began, most women were surprisingly uninhibited about expressing their opinions. Many were even proud that they had enough to recount to fill several tapes: "Puxa vida! Eu falei tudo isso?" [Heavens! I said all that?] was a frequent comment, accompanied by a pleased smile as I changed a tape. They were also pleased that their testimony was to become part of a booklet that I prepared and gave to the communities for their own use and reflection.

Although I did not reside in Santo Antônio, I spent three to four days per week there. Traveling by metro or train and bus (about a two hour trip) from what residents in the periphery call "the city" gave me an appreciation of the arduous journeys workers make each day. I was often fortunate enough to stay overnight in people's homes. I attended mass, prayer groups, novenas, retreats, *festas juninas* (street parties in June), family parties, funerals, political meetings, marches, women's group meetings, social movement meetings, and literacy classes. Whenever possible, I attended as more than simply an observer. I helped distribute food from the community purchasing project, and was "official photographer" and historian for marches and rallies. I read Bible lessons, participated in reflections, and cooked, painted, and knitted with women. These events gave me additional chances to speak informally with respondents. They allowed me to witness the interactions and reactions of members as they went about their religious and political activities. More importantly, perhaps, they drew me close to many individuals through shared experiences.

Throughout the year I was received as part of the communities of Santo Antônio. Despite the reservations of some of the local pastoral agents, the women in the CEBs accepted me as a friend, and in one case, almost as a daughter. Without the goodwill and forbearance of the respondents, this research could not have been completed. When I returned to Brazil in 1990, I found the communities to be just as open and welcoming to me. Although I was not able to re-interview all the respondents at that time, I was able to gather some valuable updated information.

Although this analysis is based on a particular case, it cannot be understood apart from the evolution of liberation theology and the Brazilian Popular Church. Chapter 2 provides a brief general overview of this history, concluding with a description of the birth of the base communities in Santo Antônio. Chapter 3 describes the characteristics of CEB members generally, as well as those interviewed. In terms of most socioeconomic characteristics, the interviewees are fairly typical urban CEB members. In addition to the more standard socioeconomic indicators, however, it is also helpful to know more about the women's roles and gender attitudes in order to understand how gender might influence their religious experiences in the CEBs. Thus, chapter 3 includes information on the women's private and public lives and their attitudes about women's roles.

Chapters 4 and 5 describe the ways in which religious experience in the CEBs is gendered, and the consequences for political mobilization and class-based consciousness-raising. Chapter 4 examines the variations in women's religious orientations, as reflected in their divergent interpretations of liberation theology. Chapter 5 then considers how common threads in these disparate religious orientations are woven together with gender-based themes to produce successful political mobilization for social movements. It argues that gender identity, rather than liberation theology, provides the "glue" that holds together a politically diverse constituency in the communities' social movements.

Finally, chapter 6 asks whether the Popular Church can help women develop strategies for personal empowerment and changing gender relations. Both opportunities for and constraints on women's personal empowerment and gender consciousness abound in the CEBs. The chapter examines differences among women who share a belief in the primacy of domestic roles and argues that their commitment to those roles is not necessarily evidence of a "lack" of feminist consciousness.

TWO

"The Midwives Were Women"

The Birth of the Popular Church
in Brazil and Santo Antônio

Leonardo and Clodovis Boff, Frei Betto, Hélder Câmara, Paulo Evaristo Arns, Pedro Casadáliga: the names of the male liberation theologians and the progressive bishops who played a key role in founding the Popular Church in Brazil are familiar to many. They developed the theory, and they formulated the pastoral plans for the *comunidades de base*. And, despite the claims of some writers, the Brazilian Popular Church could not have been born without them.[1] In a sense, these men "conceived" the People's Church: it was born of their vision of a new institution, new symbolism, and new spiritual and political commitment.

While history has recorded the names of the men who conceived a new church, however, it has generally failed to note the names of the women who brought it to life. The image of women as the "midwives" at the birth of the Popular Church is apt. For if the Boffs and Arnses and Câmaras conceived of the liberationist project, thousands of anonymous pastoral workers and laity made it a reality by creating and nurturing the base communities. While both men and women participated in these efforts, religious and lay women played an especially prominent role in many areas, including the parish of Santo Antônio. In contrast to the exclusively male roster of theologians and bishops, the list of those whose work created the CEBs includes a disproportionate number of Marias.[2]

The discovery of women's importance in the birth of the Popular Church is in some respects surprising. Although they were always numerically important in Brazilian Catholicism, women's typical activities in the pre-liberationist church—charity work, devotional societies, festivals—hardly seemed adequate preparation for the radicalizing and politicizing messages of liberation theology. Similarly, lay women had always deferred to male clerical authority and were often more deferential to the "padre" than men, yet the Popular Church would call on them as laity to take on some of his religious authority. In short, women's roles made them appear passive and conservative—an unlikely audience for a new, politically radical theology. Moreover, the new theology did not particularly go out of its way to appeal to or evangelize women. In fact, its class analysis and emphasis on the poor as workers could be seen as a "gendered" message aimed implicitly at poor men. It was, then, unclear how the female majority in the preconciliar church would fit in with the new project of liberation theology.[3]

Men dominate official and national church structures and discussions, including those related to the CEBs. As a result, the history of women's involvement in the CEBs is invisible unless one looks at the local level. An account of women's role in the local communities is crucial to retelling a more complete history. At the same time, however, the "women as midwives" image suggests how inseparable such a local history is from the changes and developments that were taking place within the larger church: women's participation facilitated and was facilitated by the new liberationist church.

The basic ideas of liberation theology are already familiar to many, and its symbolism will be discussed in more detail in chapter 4.[4] The story of the birth of the liberationist church in Latin America generally, and Brazil in particular, has also received ample attention.[5] This chapter will, therefore, describe the emergence of liberation theology and the CEBs in Brazil only briefly before proceeding to an account of the birth of the CEBs in Santo Antônio.

THE BIRTH OF THE POPULAR CHURCH IN BRAZIL

Understanding the institutional history of the Popular Church is a crucial prerequisite to interpreting the base communities. The base communities in Latin America cannot be understood apart from the institutional context because, with a few exceptions such as Nicaragua, the Popular Church and the grassroots communities are closely linked to the church hierarchy.[6] Certainly in Brazil, the CEBs were far from spontaneous lay creations. While it is true that the first CEBs or perhaps proto-CEBs antedate important developments in liberation theology, these initial experiments with new forms of lay organization and evangelization were themselves a product of institutional concerns and plans.[7] Moreover, the CEBs grew most rapidly in the 1970s, a time when liberationist bishops dominated the Brazilian hierarchy. As a result, the CEBs became closely associated with a liberationist agenda in many regions of Brazil.[8] In fact, they can be seen as the organizational form of the liberationist church.[9]

Both liberation theology and the CEBs have connections with earlier Catholic social thought (e.g., Leo XIII's 1891 encyclical *Rerum Novarum*) and lay organizations (Catholic Action in the 1930s).[10] However, the enormous social, political, and religious tumult in Brazil in the 1950s and 1960s, along with the changes wrought by the Second Vatican Council, combined to ensure that the liberationist church evolved in quite a new direction. Where the preconciliar church had stressed religious authority, personal charity, and elite political action, the liberationist church came to espouse decentralized authority, social justice, and the poor as political actors.[11]

The rapid socioeconomic changes of the 1950s brought a variety of challenges to Brazil and to the church. Some social groups benefited while others experienced increasing poverty, widening class, urban-rural, and regional divides. Populist politics stimulated worker and peasant political organization, as politicians like Getúlio Vargas and João Goulart sought to preempt left wing labor organizing while mobilizing mass political support for their nationalist, developmentalist projects. At the same time, the church was attempting to revitalize lay participation by the middle classes. It also struggled with the loss of "traditional" Catholics from strongholds like Minas Gerais and the Northeast. Often relatively unchurched due to shortages of clergy in rural areas, they increasingly embraced evangelical Protestantism or Afro-Brazilian sects as they migrated to cities (Della Cava 1989, 145). Attempts to reach these two groups—the urban middle class and the poor—came together in the Catholic students' movements, whose social projects, including the creation of peasant leagues and literacy training using Paulo Freire's consciousness-raising techniques, brought middle-class students face-to-face with poverty and proved a radicalizing experience for many (Boff 1984b, 20; Bruneau 1974, 88–92).[12] They also linked these sectors of the church with the "radical" organizing carried out by populist politicians, whose pro-worker rhetoric, though often belied by their actions, gave the military and elites pause.

The effects of industrialization and urbanization focused church elites' attention more firmly on issues of poverty and social justice and convinced many of the need for Catholic involvement in the political process, as the rising number of statements issued by the hierarchy from 1950 onward shows (Hewitt 1991, 17). At the same time, these socioeconomic developments made the church hierarchy acutely aware of the tenuous nature of its hold on the mass of believers. While the urban result was the formation of student groups, in rural areas such as Maranhão the church hierarchy began to promote decentralized rural chapels in which lay ministers would evangelize and perform some of the functions of absent clergy. The chapels were perceived solely as a means to foster a generalized sense of community and spirituality, and to provide religious orientation and celebrations for the dispersed rural communities (Adriance 1986, 58–60; Mainwaring 1986, 108). Eventually, greater lay participation was joined to social justice. The *Plano de emergência* (1962), developed by dom Hélder Câmara of Recife, proposed a pastoral strategy of base community-type groups and "sought to define priorities for future pastoral action in the social and political arenas" (Hewitt 1991, 17; Adriance 1986, 96–97 and 104–6).

Changes in the international church, crystallized in the Second Vatican Council (1962–65), reinforced and legitimized the changes in Brazil. The international church, following the encyclicals of John XXIII, for the first time clearly encouraged Catholic engagement in political life on behalf of social justice, substituting an emphasis on human responsibility for a preconciliar emphasis on submissiveness (Hewitt 1991, 16; Levine 1990, 30; Gutiérrez 1990, 12; Burdick 1993, 37–39). At the same time, liturgical reforms and encouragement of Bible study circles showed an increasing concern with opening up religious participation for the laity. And, in an important development for the future of liberation theology, John XXIII's encyclicals also opened the possibility of integrating social science analysis with religious reflection and even of "collaborating with marxism" (Levine 1990, 30).[13]

National and international trends thus reinforced the movement toward a decentralized authority structure, greater emphasis on the poor, and attention to social justice issues. The military coup of 1964, however, temporarily halted the development of a church of the poor (Hewitt 1991, 17). In the wake of the coup, political persecution of Catholic activists was widespread, and the bishops—especially the many conservative ones troubled by recent developments—did little to help (Bruneau 1974, 84; Adriance 1986, 74, 79). They continued to press for exclusively sacramental, apolitical small religious groups, however, as a means of reaching the poor and stemming Protestant encroachments. Thus for the first time in 1965, the *Plano Pastoral de Conjunto* encouraged the formation of *comunidades eclesiais de base,* CEBs. It was not until the late 1960s and early 1970s that the idea of these small groups was once again linked to the commitment to social justice, and more specifically to liberation theology.

The radicalization of the CEBs and the birth of the Popular Church depended on a rededication to social justice, rather than traditional Catholic charity, and a commitment to the poor as political actors, rather than traditional reliance on social and political elites to moralize the economic and social orders. These changes were facilitated once again by a combination of national and international events. Within Brazil, growing attacks on the church and activist clergy and Catholic laity by the military regime (1964–85) pushed the church as a whole into opposition, and brought liberationist bishops to prominence within the national hierarchy. The church began to denounce the economic ravages of capitalist development in Brazil, as well as specific attacks on church personnel. Soon São Paulo, under the leadership of the progressive archbishop dom Paulo Evaristo Arns, came to be seen as the voice of the national church. Dom Paulo led the church in its "prophetic denunciations" of economic injustice (Della Cava, 1989, 146–48). Meanwhile, the Latin American bishops' conference at Medellín, Colombia in 1968 endorsed a variety of liberationist ideas, including the concept of CEBs, the promotion of the poor as active agents of history, and the need for the regional church to commit itself to social justice. Brazilians, including Hélder Câmara, played a key role in organizing the conference. Medellín, in turn, helped to elevate liberationist bishops within Brazil from a vocal minority to dominance within the national conference.[14]

By 1974, liberationist bishops dominated the national church organizations in Brazil. In addition to a social justice agenda, they promoted a pastoral agenda centered on the formation of CEBs in various regions of the country. Two national meetings of CEBs in Vitória, ES, in 1975 and 1976 brought them to a new prominence. In their wake, São Paulo adopted two pastoral plans for the expansion of CEBs in 1976 and 1978 (Della Cava 1989, 149). The period 1974–82, which coincided with the hegemony of liberationist bishops within the national church, saw the most rapid expansion of CEBs (Mainwaring 1986, 145).

Thus, the two major aspects of the Popular Church— a social justice and activist theology and grassroots pastoral organizations—emerged separately, but were united and share a common history from the 1970s on. In addition, liberation theology and CEBs "are related as theory is to practice" (Levine 1992, 45). Liberation theology, the guiding theory of the Popular Church, finds its organizational expression in the base communities. The communities reflect not only a commitment to decentralization and democratization of religious authority, but also the fundamental shift implied in liberation theology from a preconciliar Catholic reliance on the social and political guidance of lay elites, to a new emphasis on the poor as agents of social change and as bearers of religious values.

Phillip Berryman summarizes the implications of liberation theology's fundamental concern with poverty and the poor: "liberation theology is an interpretation of Christian faith out of the experience of the poor. It is an attempt to read the Bible and key Christian doctrines with the eyes of the poor. It is at the same time an attempt to help the poor interpret their own faith in a new way" (Berryman 1987, 4–5). A number of specific consequences follow. First, an interpretation of faith from the experience of the poor not only leads to a reinterpretation of religious symbols, but also reinforces a commitment to social change and action for social justice. Second, by according the experience of the poor a privileged position—their everyday lives and insights are a unique source of religious interpretation and values—liberation theologians reconceptualize the relationship between pastoral agents and the poor. The poor are no longer just an oppressed group on whose behalf the committed Christian works. Since liberationists are to understand their faith "with the eyes of the poor," they must grant the poor themselves a large degree of authority and autonomy. As a result, the pastoral agent seeks not to act *for* or teach the poor, but rather to accompany them in their struggles. Finally, as Berryman's concluding statement suggests, liberation theologians recognize that not all popular beliefs and values are inherently liberating. Thus, they seek to help the poor interpret their religious faith in ways that affirm their humanity and their rights, motivating them to struggle for social justice. The mechanism for helping the poor to achieve this is consciousness-raising, in which lay people and pastoral agents discuss religious themes in the context of the life realities of the poor. Liberationists do not value just any participation: they want informed participation, and participation that reinforces popular empowerment and leads to social change. More clearly articulated, liberating values and empowerment through consciousness-raising should enable the poor to engage in social and political activities leading to change.

CEBs are organizations of the poor: most are located in poor rural or urban peripheral areas.[15] They encourage intense participation and lay leadership. Lay ministers may lead liturgies and perform baptisms and marriages, as well as teach catechism and lead Bible and consciousness-raising groups. Small study groups are intended to provide everyone a chance to comment, and reading the Bible in simple language while relating the stories to daily life is meant to facilitate broad participation. As a result, CEBs are uniquely suited to be the organizational form of liberation theology: the two are theoretically, as well as historically, linked.

CEBs as a vehicle for religious and political transformation and participation of and by the poor is the ideal of liberation theology. CEBs vary, however, in the extent to which they are informed by this liberationist concept. They are primarily religious organizations, and many have little direct political involvement. They vary in the extent to which they promote consciousness-raising, political activism, and even the democratization of religious authority. As Daniel Levine points out, some groups called CEBs are actually not liberationist at all, while others share a liberationist inspiration, but differ in the extent to which pastoral workers permit lay autonomy, or promote consciousness-raising along liberationist lines (Levine 1992).

Brazilian CEBs have mostly been liberationist in inspiration.[16] Santo Antônio is one region in which liberationist theology clearly influenced pastoral strategies. There, CEBs are not only numerous, but also have a decidedly liberationist orientation. They have been committed not only to consciousness-raising, but also to promoting political action through social movements and more traditional political channels, such as electoral politics.

Thus the Popular Church generally and CEBs specifically constitute a new departure in Catholicism, although one with roots traceable to earlier developments in the religion's history. The commitment to lay participation and democratization of authority, the emphasis on social justice, and finally, the active promotion of the poor as agents of historical change all constitute what John Burdick calls "new branches" from Catholicism's "familiar roots" (Burdick 1993, 1). Even without the promotion of social justice issues and political activism per se, the Popular Church offers new forms of participation, a new democratic ethos, and the possibility of personal empowerment and radically altered worldviews for the poor. The crucial question raised by the CEBs, then, is how they have affected the religious, social, and political perspectives of their participants.

As the term "base community" suggests, the liberationist church is committed to mobilizing and enhancing the religious and political participation of the "base." Liberation theology's focus on poverty and its commitment to valuing the experiences of average people leads to a definition of that "base" in terms of two characteristics. In social terms, the "base" is the poor, those at the bottom of what liberationists like to call the "social pyramid." In religious terms, it is the laity, those at the base of the church structure.

Liberationists, at least initially, saw the CEBs as organizations of the laity of a particular social class, the poor. Thus the expectation was that these new organizations with their new values would raise class consciousness. They did not generally expect CEBs to represent the "base" of a patriarchal gender system. Yet many CEBs are characteristically not only organizations of the poor and the laity, but also of women. Male theologians and pastoral agents did not conceptualize the Popular Church as a female church. As the concept of the CEBs took on flesh in real parishes and neighborhoods, however, they frequently did so primarily through the efforts of women. In many regions, including Santo Antônio, the bishops' and theologians' ambitious liberationist project would have been stillborn had not women been present to give the idea of CEBs life. In doing so, women have given it their own distinctive mark.

WOMEN AND THE BIRTH OF THE POPULAR CHURCH:
SANTO ANTÔNIO, 1980-90

The interaction between pastoral agents and laity in CEB formation is clear in the history of Santo Antônio. Despite the area's poverty and lack of services, CEBs did not emerge spontaneously from the religious experiences of the poor. Santo Antônio, unlike many other equally impoverished areas, produced a well-organized, active, and relatively strong Popular Church because it was located in an unusually propitious context. The archdiocese of São Paulo, which until 1989 included Santo Antônio, was headed by dom Paul Evaristo Arns, a leading national spokesman for the liberationist church. Santo Antônio is also located in the diocese of São Miguel Paulista. From 1975 to 1989, a period encompassing the heyday of the liberationist church in Brazil as a whole, São Miguel Paulista was headed by Bishop Angélico Sândalo Bernardino, a fiery proponent of the option for the poor.[17]

São Miguel Paulista attracted many pastoral agents committed to a preferential option for the poor and to the development of CEBs. Many, although certainly not all, pastoral workers in the region prior to 1989 shared dom Angélico's views and commitments. Clergy in this region were on average somewhat younger than those in other dioceses. Many were of an age to have been educated in the atmosphere of openness and inquiry which followed the Second Vatican Council and witnessed the development of liberation theology (Hewitt 1985, 179). According to a survey of parish priests in São Paulo, they fell into the age group which showed the most acceptance of both the option for the poor and its political implications, such as the establishment of socialism or a "popular regime." Many such priests hold pre-1989 Nicaragua, a revolutionary regime with ties to the Popular Church, to be a relevant political example (Pierucci 1984, 486, 327, 351).

With such pastoral leadership, São Miguel Paulista witnessed an exceptional level of CEB growth through the mid-
1980s, a period in which CEBs began to decline in similar regions of the archdiocese. In 1986 the diocese had 47 parishes
with an estimated 159 CEBs, approximately 30 of these in
Santo Antônio. This parish and its surrounding area, Itaim
Paulista, stood out even in this unusually liberationist diocese
as an activist, dynamic center of CEB growth.[18]

The CEBs in Santo Antônio began as a result of the efforts
of liberationist pastoral agents who arrived in the area at about
the same time that dom Angélico became bishop. A group of
young priests and nuns led by an Italian priest, Padre Chico,
arrived in Santo Antônio with a strong commitment to liberation theology and the formation of CEBs in 1975 (interview,
Apr. 1986). An older Brazilian priest, Padre Angelo, also arrived in 1975, having previously worked in the Zona Sul of
São Paulo. The Zona Sul experienced earlier CEB growth than
the Zona Leste and was at the time considered more radical
and "advanced" (Rede Mulher interview, Jan. 1984). A nun,
Sister Terezinha, who had previous experience working with
CEBs in Rio de Janeiro, arrived in the parish in 1978 (interview,
Aug. 1986).

The priests and nuns who arrived in the mid- to late 1970s
expressed their commitment to a preferential option for the
poor in a variety of ways. They use a liberationist analysis of
the primary source of the Brazilian working class's oppression.
They attempt to transmit the religious and political discourses
developed in liberation theology. The priests, in particular, are
in a position to offer church resources to support and legitimize social movements and other political activities.[19] Some,
such as Padre Chico and Sister Nilce, also openly sided with
and encouraged support of the Workers' Party (PT). Chico,
for example, has strong contacts with both the PT and its related trade union organization. He has actively promoted the

Pastoral Operária, the workers' pastoral which is identified with the "radical line" of the church. Indeed, according to one of the PO coordinators for the archdiocese, Itaim Paulista has an exceptionally strong PO, thanks largely to Padre Chico's activism (interview, Sept. 1986).

The priests' role in legitimizing the communities, their religious orientation, and the social movements is an important one. Many social movements and events in the communities' history are inextricably linked in participants' minds with the presence of particularly charismatic priests, as evidence in chapters 4 and 5 suggests. One young priest, a young man from the area, was killed in an automobile accident in the early 1980s. His picture still hung on the walls of many CEB homes in 1986, and he was regarded by some as somewhat of a martyr because of his support for the communities. Padre Chico's reassignment to northern Brazil in 1986 was keenly felt in the CEBs, many of whose leaders continued to rely on Chico for advice and support by telephone or letter.

The role of women religious also bears some special attention here, for in many respects they are more integrated into the daily life of the communities than are the priests. Madeleine Adriance states that women religious working in the CEBs outnumber priests by three to one in Maranhão, making them overwhelmingly "the largest group of pastoral agents involved with CEBs" (Adriance 1991, 299). Moreover, there is a sense in which women religious are more integrated into the lives of the communities than priests. Patrick Peritore cites a woman lay worker in Bahia who says, "Women base workers in the church are much more efficient than male religious; they are more easily accepted, create affectual links more easily, and can mobilize women who are the church's main clientele. . . . Base work with the people is women's work, men couldn't stand it" (Peritore 1990, 151–52). Although I do not have exact information on the ratio of nuns to priests in Santo Antônio, it is correct that women religious outnumber priests in the area. The priests also must divide their time among all the CEBs and often can only say mass in each once a month. They are based at the parish, which is only loosely connected with any particular community, while the nuns live and participate in *vilas* or *bairros* with CEBs. The nuns are thus more likely to be involved in the CEB's routine activities, as Adriance found in Maranhão (Adriance 1991, 302–3). At prayer meetings, Bible study, catechism, even the weekly sewing and literacy classes, the women religious are present. They are often in daily contact with women lay leaders, and their role in transmitting liberationist ideas includes focusing reflection on the themes of the material liberation of the poor and the role of Christ as their historical liberator at numerous meetings, not just at mass (field notes, Mar., April, Aug., Nov. 1986).

These liberationist pastoral workers—both priests and nuns—laid the groundwork for the formation of CEBs in the parish.[20] As they did so, they encountered an active laity comprised overwhelmingly of poor women. In Santo Antônio as elsewhere in São Paulo, women became the organizational basis of the communities. They continued to be their backbone throughout the 1980s.

The pastoral agents were interested in promoting consciousness-raising through Bible study. The first group that began meeting for Bible reflection consisted of about fifty women catechists. The reflections gradually moved away from the sacramental to focus more on local problems (interviews, Apr., 1986, and Rede Mulher, January 1984). Six large *núcleos* emerged from the group of catechists, and through these groups the CEBs spread. One woman recalled:

> The first thing that happened here, we didn't have a community. We met in houses. We were a group of women, and

we met in our houses. And then that group of women began to grow, and it was growing so well that we formed several groups. It kept growing, with groups here, groups there. We had a general meeting every month, but in somebody's house. Then the purchase of the land came up, and we began to build (the community center). . . . (interview, Aug. 1986, Aimoré)

From 1977 to 1981, most CEBs followed a similar path culminating in the building of a community center.

An activist in another CEB recalls the building of the local church as follows:

Ten years ago, the *cúria* gave this land to us. And we were just women who met to reflect on the gospel. And they offered this land to us, and we accepted, but we didn't know what to do. Then, we began to clear off the brush, we got enthusiastic . . . and *then we managed to get the men involved through the construction.* We began a fund drive for the construction, and I think that motivated us, because to accomplish things, we had to struggle. (interview, Apr. 1986, emphasis added)

According to these and other lay women and pastoral agents in the region, men were only marginally involved in the formation and day-to-day activities of the CEBs from the beginning. Women were the first recruits and organizers, and while they did sometimes "manage to get the men involved," it was largely their initiatives that built the local churches.

By 1980–81, most areas of the parish had simple community centers, which serve as both churches and meeting places, the focal points of the CEBs. The number of CEBs continued to grow, with the newest inaugurated in 1986 (interview, Apr. 1986). As the groups grew, the variety of activities expanded.

Pastoral agents attempted to promote lay leadership and con-sciousness-raising activities in particular. They also encouraged and helped to organize a variety of social movements.

Chica's recollection of the trajectory of her participation in the CEB indicates the variety of activities the groups typi-cally undertook once they became established:

> When the nuns came, they had meetings in the houses. They invited me, and I went. We didn't have a church then, we went to mass at the parish. Then came the land here, and we did everything possible to build the (community's) church. Then came the council, and my name was put forward. . . . So after some time, they created the coun-cil. Then the priest said the council had to assume cer-tain responsibilities. In terms of struggles, and within the church. And next thing I knew, I was in the ministry of bap-tism! I still am, up to today. And then through the church, the struggles (social movements) began emerging. . . . (Dec. 1986)

Chica's testimony outlines a common pattern of development. Most of Santo Antônio's CEBs initially formed a community council to organize activities. Catechists' groups continued to operate, but now with a revised, liberationist-inspired cate-chism. Liturgy groups were formed to organize and conduct religious celebrations on Sundays when the priest could not be present. Later, other lay ministries were created to con-duct baptism and marriage preparation classes, as well as to lead community celebrations of these sacraments. Diocesan and archdiocesan pastoral agents with an expertise in leading Bible study groups were called in to give short courses on spe-cific topics. Eventually, these sporadically offered Bible courses were supplemented by the formation of *grupos de rua*. These groups, organized by street throughout the CEB, meet weekly for prayer, reflection on Biblical passages or prepared materials, and consciousness-raising. Finally, the groups became involved in diverse local social movements, demanding municipal attention to issues from garbage and asphalt to daycare, health centers, and street lights. In 1982, the CEBs in Santo Antônio also participated in support efforts for the striking factory workers in São Paulo's industrial suburbs.[21]

In all of these groups and efforts, a common element is the centrality of participation by women in the CEBs' Mothers' Clubs. Most of the communities emerged from the groups of women catechists and their offshoots in the neighborhoods. In an effort to expand participation, these groups often organized Mothers' Clubs as well as specifically reflection-oriented groups. The Mothers' Clubs hoped to attract women by offering a combination of instruction in skills, usually sewing or crocheting, and prayer and reflection.

Iracema was successfully recruited into active participation in the community by just such a group:

> I had a life where I did not get out of the house much, you know? It was that struggle, five children and all small—that was my life. And I found it difficult, too, because I didn't know what participation was, what the base community was. . . . When Padre Angelo said we should get involved in our streets, get a group together, I thought it would be so difficult. I wanted to do something, but I thought it would be so difficult to get out. Until one day I got my courage up and went to the group, even though it was knitting and crocheting, and I didn't like that. I still don't! But I liked the reflection, and getting the women together and conversing, and from there I got started. (Apr. 1986)

Many women's stories are similar, and the Mothers' Clubs became such an integral part of the CEBs that their story is largely the story of the communities. Women, and especially those in the Mothers' Clubs, are recognized as the force behind Santo Antônio's CEBs, as Sonia Alvarez noted in another region of São Paulo as well (Alvarez 1991b, 21–22).

In each community I heard some variation of Zélia's description: "as I've said, if the women stop in the community, the community stops, no? It's women who make the church, really, liturgy, catechism, all of that and more. And the church, the community would maybe even end up closed" (Oct. 1986).[22] At another time she said, "Without the Mothers' Club, there would be no CEBs." Observation and the testimony of other women bear her out to a large extent. Women are disproportionately represented in the CEBs generally, but they are even more overrepresented among the most intensely active participants. Ministries and liturgy groups are organized by Mothers' Club members. In most communities, the council overlaps heavily with the Mothers' Club. The latter, rather than the council per se, is usually recollected as the focus of organizing efforts for the various social movements.

This is not to say that men are not involved in the communities, nor that they have not also been key participants in their organization and development. Aside from the critical role played by male pastoral workers, most communities cite at least one or two men among their founders and leaders. Men constitute about one third of community members. In CEBs throughout São Paulo in 1984, they constituted about a third of council members as well, a figure that rose to over 50 percent by 1988 (Hewitt 1991, 64).[23]

In Santo Antônio, however, women appear to shoulder a larger burden in running the daily activities of the groups, and, in addition to being a numerical majority, they participate more intensively in group life. Twenty-four people participated in one CEB's annual assembly to assess progress and set priorities, for example. Only two of the participants were male. Half of the women present were regular participants in the Mothers' Club (field notes, Sept. 1986).

One pastoral agent in the region stated that very few men had ever participated in the groups and that generally all the work of the communities was carried out by women (Oct. 1986). Very few of the weekly prayer groups, the *grupos de rua,* are run by men, for example (Oct. 1986). In one community when I asked if men participated in the groups, the following dialogue ensued:

> (First speaker): More women than men here. Men, there are very few. Well, mine is on a weekday during the day, no? . . . But even if we do it on a weekend, the men don't participate even if they're home. It's more women. Some young people, children might participate. . . . Now, in other groups, I don't know if any men participate.
>
> (Second speaker): Rodrigo, Rogerio, Celso. [Laughter] Just those men!
>
> (To me:) Those are our kids!(Aug. 1986).

Indeed, an informal survey of *grupos de rua* in Santo Antônio found that only 10 percent of participants were men ("Aos animadores" 1986, 127–28).

Despite prominent exceptions, male presence in the CEBs is largely restricted to attendance at mass (Oct. 1986). Moreover, according to pastoral agents, men tend to use the CEBs as stepping stones to other forms of activism. One man who had been prominent in the formation of Iracema's CEB became an activist in the metro operators' union, for example. Although he continued to be a nominal member of the community council, he no longer attended meetings or other activities aside from mass by 1986. A pastoral agent with the *Pastoral Operária,* the Workers' Pastoral, noted a similar phenomenon in that organization. Men, she noted, often moved on from the PO to unions or other forms of political work, while women militants tended to keep up their involvement in church activities despite taking on new ones as well (Sept. 1986). Similarly, another nun in the area described two parallel forms of activism in the region: a masculine movement located in the unions and political parties, and a feminine one located largely in the church and its sponsored social movements (Oct. 1986).

Santo Antônio's experience may not be representative. Elsewhere, men appear to have played a prominent and continuing role in the communities. Rural CEBs, especially, may have a more balanced gender composition.[24] But Santo Antônio is far from unique. In interviews conducted throughout the Eastern and Southern Zones of São Paulo by the feminist group Rede Mulher, women commonly recounted the importance of the Mothers' Clubs to the functioning of the local CEB and social movements. As one activist, not herself a member of the CEB, said, "The church, the movements, the Mothers' Club . . . it's all the same women" (Rede Mulher interview, n.d.). A woman from another community responded to a query about whether she was describing the founding of her CEB or her Mothers' Club echoed Zélia's statement above, saying simply, "The Mothers' Club is the church . . . we were going to found the Mothers' Club and celebrate mass" (Rede Mulher interview, Apr. 1984).

CONCLUSIONS

The birth of the Popular Church in Santo Antônio could not have occurred outside the context of the development of a liberationist orientation in the Brazilian church as a whole. Priests, the local bishop, and the archbishop of Santo Antônio acted on these liberationist ideals to begin founding the CEBs. As they took shape on the ground, however, the CEBs quickly became not only organizations of the poor but also organizations of women. The Popular Church in Santo Antônio, and perhaps in Brazil as a whole, would have been stillborn if not for the labor and participation of thousands of religious and lay women.

Liberation theology has been centrally concerned with the liberation of the poor and the oppressed. It has not, until quite recently, specifically included women in those categories. The CEBs were conceived of as organizations of the poor, and liberation theology itself and consciousness-raising generally aimed to raise issues of poverty and social class, not gender. Of course, the women in the CEBs are poor: their social and economic conditions give them ample grounds to respond to the liberationist project on its own terms. But while many aspects of life for the poor are common to men and women, in other respects poverty can be considered "gendered," a fact that may have implications for the way that the CEBs and the Popular Church developed in Santo Antônio.

THREE

Being Poor, Being Female

Socioeconomic and Gender Characteristics of CEB Members

By now it has become commonplace to speak of CEBs as communities of the poor, but just what does it mean to be poor in urban Brazil? What experiences and opportunities shape the lives of those poor people who choose to join CEBs? This chapter focuses first on the common experiences of poor men and women: migration and life in a poor urban environment. It gives a sense of the experiences shared by the urban poor in Brazil, but also indicates some ways in which poor CEB members differ from their neighbors, and from the stereotype of the liberationist church. Next, since gender appears to be a critical factor in the self-selection of urban CEB members, it asks how the experiences of poor women differ from those of men. Unpacking the category of gender to see just what roles and attitudes are characteristic of women in CEBs is a crucial prerequisite to understanding the specific channels through which gender shapes their experience of poverty and may affect their religious and political activities.

WORLDS OF THE POOR: THE SHARED EXPERIENCES OF MIGRATION AND URBAN POVERTY

When liberationists specify who "the poor" in the CEBs are, they often cite migration, manual labor, unemployment or underemployment, low income, residence in unsafe housing and in areas with poor infrastructure as characteristic of CEB members.[1] In general terms, such descriptions are fairly accurate. Indeed, they are implied by the fact that most urban CEBs are located in poor areas on the edges of the metropolitan center (Demo and Calsing 1981, 20).[2] Ninety percent of São Paulo's CEBs are located in the city's poor periphery, where they also achieved the fastest growth (Hewitt 1985, 100–102). Peripheral neighborhoods are characterized by a high degree of rural-to-urban migration, low-skill labor and low income levels, and poor living conditions, including a lack of infrastructure.

A more concrete picture based on accounts from and descriptions of life in Itaim Paulista and in the particular communities that comprise the parish of Santo Antônio will clarify the conditions in which CEBs emerge and develop. CEB members share many conditions of urban poverty with their neighbors, but it is also important to point out ways in which they differ from nonmembers. In general, while CEB members are poor, they are not among the poorest residents of the urban periphery and are even slightly above average in income.

Migration to São Paulo

Itaim Paulista was still quite separate from metropolitan São Paulo as late as the 1950s. Nearly thirty miles distant from the city center, Itaim was rural; even neighboring São Miguel Paulista, closer to metropolitan São Paulo, was an unincorporated small town. These conditions changed as the area's population grew rapidly from the 1940s through the 1980s, mostly due to migration from the rural states of Minas Gerais and northeastern Brazil. Many migrants settled in Itaim in order to work at the Nitroquímica factory, which continues to be an important employer (Caldeira 1984, 31, 39).

By 1980, nearly 80 percent of São Miguel Paulista's economically active population over age twenty was composed of persons born outside of the metropolitan area (Caldeira 1984,

88).[3] Since most urban peripheral areas experienced similar histories, it is not surprising that many urban CEB members are migrants. In peripheral CEBs throughout São Paulo, W. E. Hewitt found that 53.6 percent of members were born outside the city (Hewitt 1985, 120). An even higher percentage of those interviewed in the parish of Santo Antônio in Itaim were migrants: just three of thirty women—the youngest interviewed—were born in the city. Thus active members in Santo Antônio's CEBs resemble the proportion of migrants in the general population.[4]

CEB members in Santo Antônio come from typical areas of outmigration. They were born in the rural "interior" of São Paulo state (three); in neighboring Minas Gerais, a highly traditional and "Catholic" state (five); or in the impoverished states of the Northeast and the Central West, such as Pernambuco, Alagoas, Sergipe, Bahia, Paraíba, and Goiás.[5] Almost all described having grown up in the countryside.[6]

Life in the countryside meant hard work for men and women, for they worked side by side in the fields. A fifty-five-year-old woman from Minas recalled simply, "I always worked in the fields (*na roça*)" (interview, Aug. 1986) while thirty-year-old Cleide from São Paulo described the difficult life of the small Brazilian farmer: "I also lived in the countryside, so I know. My father also worked as a field hand for others. . . . And when we worked in the fields, we got up at 5:30 in the morning, weeded all day long and came home at 6:00 in the evening covered with clay" (Aug. 1986). The difficult work, along with isolation, limited opportunities for rural dwellers. A fifty-nine-year-old woman from the interior of São Paulo said that as a youngster she had little awareness of politics because "I was in the fields (*na roça*), a day laborer (*bóia-fria*). I don't know if you know Itu? Have you been there? I'm from there, Itu, except that we didn't live in the city. We lived on a small farm (*sítio*)" (Oct. 1986). Similarly, Cleide was unable to complete her education because: "I lived on a farm in the interior. At that time, there was no high school, only primary school, and so I was never able to finish" (Aug. 1986).

Despite its possible long-term benefits, migration exacts a high price, both financially and psychologically. Cleide recalled her family's arrival in São Paulo city:

> When I arrived in São Paulo, my husband and I had just one daughter. Well, we arrived, as the saying goes, with one hand in front and the other behind. Without any money at all. We stayed in one person's house, ate at another's, slept at another's. We didn't have money for rent. When we got jobs, we couldn't find a place where we could afford to live. . . . Then an acquaintance arranged a little, bitty room (*desse tamanhazinho*) for us to stay in and we stayed. I did whatever work I could find. I did washing because that was the way it had to be. (Aug. 1986)

When Fátima arrived from Bahía with her husband and son in 1968, their first residence was a church-run charitable institution. Maria Angela recalled, "I was so needy, I needed bread to give my kids. With my husband sick, I had to depend on others, you see? I was completely dependent on others" (Nov. 1986). Her husband's inability to find a job led to his growing alcoholism and finally to his temporary internment in a mental hospital not long after they arrived in São Paulo from Minas Gerais.

These stories give a sense of some of the transitions and difficulties experienced by migrants. Just such stories have led some authors, including Edward Cleary and João Carlos Petrini, to suggest that CEBs may provide a way for recent migrants to ease their transition to an urban life fraught not only with economic difficulty, but also with urban problems such as drugs, crime, and family disintegration (Cleary 1985, 108; Petrini 1984, 37–38).[7]

Yet while most CEB members in Santo Antônio are migrants, few joined the groups until they were well established in the city. This may prove Cecilia Mariz's point that CEBs require a degree of economic security and free time for active participation (Mariz 1989, 86). Three exceptional cases contrast with the stories above, highlighting the fact that freedom from day-to-day survival issues facilitates incorporation into a CEB for recent migrants.

Maria dos Anjos recalled:

> A sister of mine came ahead through some cousins, and through her, I came. My sisters were all married. I was the last, and I came through my sister. And when I got to her house, my brother-in-law said, "There's no entertainment here. The entertainment we have is a church just being built." That was eighteen years ago. He said, "At home you could do anything, you were with your parents. But here, you're going to need more control!" . . . So I started to participate with that invitation! (Oct. 1986)

Maria dos Anjos's participation was motivated partly by her brother-in-law's perception that church was the only proper entertainment for his unmarried charge. It was also facilitated by the fact that she joined an already-established household. Similarly, Eloisa came from Bahia to watch her daughter's two children while the daughter and son-in-law worked. Like Maria dos Anjos, economically free and looking for an appropriate place to spend free time, Eloisa joined the CEB's women's group to "make friends" (Oct. 1986). The third exception, Joselina, migrated with eight of her thirteen children, and she managed the household while they worked. Her numerous children earned enough to free her from working outside the home, enabling her to join the church.

In contrast, most of the women in Santo Antônio joined the CEBs after having become well established in the area, lending credence to Mariz's finding that people join CEBs *after* becoming economically stable enough to afford the time, effort, and even resources CEB participation demands.[8] The precarious life of a recent migrant usually does not permit activism. Like Cleide and Maria Angela, many recent migrants must work extremely hard to make do; each day's income, and perhaps even where one will sleep, is uncertain. As Cleide recalled, "There in Ermelindo (where she first lived in São Paulo), I didn't participate. Because when I arrived from the interior, it was tough. You come here from the interior, you arrive, and end up just working, working" (Aug. 1986). Lack of friends may prevent recent migrants from learning of CEBs as well. In contrast, the women active in Santo Antônio's CEBs were already living in Itaim for anywhere from seven or eight years to as much as fifteen or sixteen years when the CEBs in Santo Antônio were beginning to form in the mid-1970s.[9]

Migration is an important formative experience for CEB members and for all residents of the periphery. They recall both the relative tranquility and freedom from modern urban problems of the countryside, as well as its limited opportunities and demanding work. They have often experienced desperate urban poverty as well, particularly immediately after arriving in the city.

Urban Poverty and Daily Life

Frei Betto, a theologian with many years of experience working with São Paulo's CEBs, characterizes their members as "people who work with their own hands (the popular classes): housewives, workers, the underemployed, youths and employees in the service sector, in the urban periphery . . ." (Betto 1981, 17).[10] He adds that the average CEB member is semiliterate, earns less than three or four minimum salaries, and resides in rundown rental housing or in a *favela,* or shantytown (Betto 1981, 19).

All of the characteristics Betto describes are associated with the "popular classes." A large gap, however, separates the *favelado* who subsists on one minimum salary and the factory worker who lives in a functional house and must get by on three or four minimum salaries, though both are poor. As it turns out, the urban poverty conjured up by television images of *favelas* in Rio de Janeiro is not typical of most CEB members, although they *are* poor.

CEB members are rarely drawn from the truly destitute *favelados*. Pastoral workers from the eastern, southern, and western zones of São Paulo all stressed the virtual impossibility of recruiting *favelados* for CEB participation, citing a variety of impediments ranging from the *favelados'* greater propensity to convert to evangelical Protestantism, to the transient residency patterns of *favelas*.[11] A survey of the ABC region of Grande São Paulo supports this conclusion, finding higher rates of CEB participation correlated positively with skilled employment, higher income, and residence in a working class neighborhood as opposed to a *favela* (Ricco 1984, 129–132).[12] Similarly, a 1994 national survey indicated that CEB self-identifiers were poor, but not the poorest of the poor (Pierucci and Prandi 1995, 32).[13]

Betto's ballpark estimate of income—three to four minimum salaries—seems fairly accurate: nearly three quarters (71.6 percent) of São Paulo CEB members were employed in blue-collar professions, and only about one quarter (23.7 percent) of CEB members earned more than five minimum salaries (Hewitt 1985, 120).[14] These figures suggest that those drawn to the base communities come from the relatively better-off strata of the poor. For example, nearly one-quarter of CEB members earn above *five* minimum salaries, while only one quarter of the population of Itaim Paulista earn above *three* minimum salaries.

CEB members in Santo Antônio share the characteristics of CEB members throughout São Paulo. In terms of employment, for example, 78 percent of husbands or male household heads are blue-collar workers. They include painters, electricians, and workers in chemical and other factories. Exceptions include a public school teacher and two men who own small local shops.[15] Most of the women in the CEBs describe themselves as housewives and, as we shall see in more detail below, women's class status is generally ascribed through their male relatives. When women do work, however, as 37 percent did at the time of the interviews, they also typically do informal sector or blue-collar work, as maids, factory workers, or sewing independently or on a piecework basis.[16]

Some sense of the range of family income can be gained by looking at key cases. The family widely acknowledged within the community as among the most affluent, for example, is that of a retired electrician who owns his own home and three small rental properties. Their current income is about five minimum salaries, depending on rental income, but would have been higher when he was still employed (Sept. 1986). Eloisa, a more typical member, lives in a rented house with her two grandchildren, daughter, and son-in-law, a factory worker who earns three minimum salaries. Their total family income may reach five minimum salaries (Oct. 1986). One of the poorest families consists of two elderly women who subsist on about two minimum salaries income from retirement benefits. They live with an irregularly employed daughter and several grandchildren.

Despite their relative well-being, CEB members share many inconveniences and burdens of life in the urban periphery with their poorer neighbors. A brief tour through Itaim Paulista reveals the difficulties of life in a peripheral urban area even for the better-off men and women. These aspects of daily life affect men and women in much the same way.

Itaim's main thoroughfare is the Estrada Rio-São Paulo, called Avenida Marechal Tito. This is a busy commercial street, lined with factories, shops, and *lanchonetes* or snack bars. Even on this main avenue, however, the signs of Itaim's relative poverty are clear. The shops are fewer and more poorly stocked than those in neighboring São Miguel, a slightly wealthier working class region. There are no supermarkets in Itaim, for example, and much shopping is done in tiny shops off the main road—often little more than storefronts—which cater to the tastes and income of the clientele. Many sell typical northeastern foods, for example, and most carry only a little merchandise, generally of low quality.

On either side of the busy, multi-lane Estrada are the *vilas* and *jardins*—the smaller neighborhoods—that comprise Itaim. Those lying north, between the Estrada and the Tietê River, are poorer than those to the south. The area also grows poorer as one proceeds east, to the neighborhoods known collectively as "the Camargos," which lie practically on the edge of the metropolitan district.

Despite some apparent differences in wealth and the presence of *favelas* in some neighborhoods, most *jardins* and *vilas* in the parish of Santo Antônio are fairly established working class neighborhoods. Although many people do live in decrepit rental housing, as Betto's description suggests, many others own modest but well-constructed homes. Early migrants to the region have been able gradually to build and improve their homes themselves.[17] Several interviewees, for example, recalled that when they arrived in Itaim Paulista in the early 1960s, they found it "full of woods and brush," which they cleared themselves in order to build their homes (Apr., Oct. 1986).

The result of the migrants' efforts can be seen in homes like the one built by Iracema's family, one of the wealthier in the community. A cement wall and wrought-iron gate surround the family's *quintal,* a front yard with a few trees, a driveway, and a carport. The cement-block house is all on one floor. The small living room is simply but neatly furnished with a sofa and arm chair, a coffee table, bookshelves filled with books, pictures, and the television. Three bedrooms accommodate Iracema and her husband, one of two daughters, three sons, and frequent visitors from Minas Gerais.[18] The bathroom consists of a sink, commode, and an open shower. The kitchen has a sink, gas stove, and refrigerator, as well as some cupboards, Iracema's sewing machine, and a large table for the family. The back yard, also enclosed, is dominated by a large mango tree and includes a small outbuilding sometimes used by one or two of the sons as a bedroom.

Iracema's family has been successful, and many in the CEBs only aspire to own such a home, which they may be in the process of building in a nearby area. Meanwhile, many rent houses similar in structure to Iracema's, but often smaller. Parents and children or grandparents and grandchildren may sleep in the same room, as in Maria Angela and Eloisa's families. Some have no living room, so the common room is the kitchen, which may also include a bed or two. Most have a least a small separate room for the couch and television. Televisions, stoves, and refrigerators—generally old and of poor quality— are common possessions: 81.3 percent of families in a neighboring area of Itaim had televisions, according to a study in the early 1980s (Caldeira 1984, 111). Telephones, however, are a mark of distinction. Iracema's family is one of the few in the community with a telephone.

Despite the relative success of families like Iracema's, their residence in a poor peripheral area means that, in addition to the lower level of consumption and difficulties of shopping alluded to earlier, they share many problems with *favelados* living in shanties. Aside from a few main streets, for example, most roads in Itaim are unpaved. When it rains in the winter, roads turn to red mud that can trap cars. In the summer, they raise clouds of dust. Waste water also runs in the streets, and garbage that is rarely collected piles up in open lots. Even the lot around the local elementary school is rimmed with garbage along the fence. Rats run from the garbage-strewn lots.

Lack of street lights also makes the area conducive to crime, which is endemic. Almost every interview conducted in Santo Antônio included reference to local crimes. Residents warn visitors about traveling in the area after dark, describing muggings that occurred at bus stops or on public transportation that the visitor will be using. Most interviewees had stories of friends and family members who had been mugged or raped, and crime is a constant topic of conversation among women in the CEB. Despite the crime, there are no policemen to be seen in Itaim.

These conditions add further daily stress and burdens to lives that are already made difficult by low and uncertain incomes. At least temporary unemployment is common, and job loss is a constant worry for even the relatively well-employed. Moreover, inflation often makes it difficult to make do even with a regular wage, with the result that more and more family members must work to contribute to family income. Brazilian inflation, which has historically been high, ran at three-digit levels in the 1980s and early 1990s. The government responded with a series of austerity plans inspired by the International Monetary Fund. Aimed at curbing inflation, the plans often produced unemployment while leaving prices untouched. All the CEBs in Santo Antônio reported that they had recently lost women activists who had to go to work to supplement their family income due to inflation or a husband's unemployment.

Daily life in Itaim or any peripheral area, even for the relatively well-off like the CEB members, is exhausting physically and emotionally. Men and women experience the effects of overcrowded homes, crime, health hazards, mud, and dust. At times, they may also share the precarious transport and often work in exploitative conditions. But while women and men share many daily realities of life in the periphery, a gender-based division of labor means that they share some of them unevenly.

THE WORLD OF POOR WOMEN: STRUGGLES IN
AND FOR THE PRIVATE SPHERE

Feminist theorists argue that poor men and women experience the world in substantially different ways. The difference, they suggest, stems from the division between public and private spheres, and the identification of men with the former and women with the latter. In a gender-based division of labor, men and women fill significantly different roles: men are the breadwinners outside the home and the "public" representative of the family, and women are the caregivers in the home, concerned more with reproduction and all it entails—cooking, cleaning, nursing—than with production.

In Brazil, as in Latin America generally, the public-private distinction has been marked, although perhaps more so in cultural norms than in actual practice. Perhaps as a legacy of a pre-twentieth-century patriarchal tradition, including laws and customs that excluded women from politics and confined them as much as possible to the private sphere, Brazilian culture distinguishes strongly between the house (*a casa*) and the street (*a rua*) (da Matta 1991, Freire 1963, Hahner 1990). Women are identified as belonging properly to the house: women taking part in a public activity (especially a political one) in the street or square may be taunted as "women of the street" and told to "go home" where they belong (field notes, Aug. 1986).

Many feminist writers argue that Brazilian Catholicism reinforces this exclusion from the public sphere (e.g., Schmink 1981, 130–31).[19] One of the main factors cited in this argument is *marianismo,* a complex web of beliefs about the Virgin Mary and devotional practices centered on her (Stevens 1973, 91–92). The term *marianismo,* however, is also applied to a feminine inverse of *machismo,* a social norm that contributes to the low status of women, especially within the public realm (Campbell 1982, 21). Catholic images associated with Mary—

suffering motherhood, purity, and moral superiority, for example—become part of the cultural norm of the ideal woman.
Societies with a strong Marian religious strain share a cultural model of womanhood that simultaneously subordinates
women and exults them as semidivine, particularly in their role
as mothers (Stevens 1973, 94, 96).

Whether religious *marianismo* is a consequence or a source
of larger patterns of cultural attitudes about gender cannot
be known. But certainly Mary has been used as a model of
women's domesticity and passivity with respect to the public,
"male" sphere, and this model is often conveyed through special Marian societies. In the 1950s and 1960s, the Legion of
Mary, Daughters of Mary, and other Marian devotional groups
were exceptionally widespread in Brazil (Perry and Echeverria
1988, 255). Their primary constituency was female, and their
message emphasized Mary's example of virginity, motherhood,
and long-suffering patience and self-abnegation for women
(Azzi 1984, 100–103). In fact, many of the women now in
CEBs were influenced by these devotional groups. Nearly one-
third were Daughters of Mary or *legionárias* in their youth.[20]

In real life, of course, public and private cannot be so
neatly divided as models of home-and-street or the *marianista*
ideal demand. Both men and women are part of families and
all participate somewhat in "public" sphere activities such as
work or politics. Poor women will probably have to enter the
world of extradomestic wage labor for at least some time at
some point in their lives: the classic model of the family in
which women remain in the home is simply not a viable economic reality for most Brazilians.[21] Women's contact with the
state and politics will include not only voting—compulsory in
Brazil—but also perhaps dealing with government bureaucrats
on issues like health coverage, school enrollment, and so on.

The separation of public and private spheres for the poor
in Brazil should not be exaggerated. The boundaries between

"men's" and "women's" realms are certainly permeable. Nonetheless, while poor women certainly cross into "male," public sphere activities, the fact remains that they do so sporadically, tentatively, and usually out of necessity. Teresa Caldeira summarizes findings of a study conducted in the Zona Leste of São Paulo: "To be a woman means to construct one's identity and define one's principal role within the family; it means, upon seeking a place in the world, to refer in the first place to the domestic group, and not to any other social institution" (Caldeira 1984, 148, my translation). For poor women, the private sphere remains the primary source of roles and identity.

This fact, and the division of labor it implies, differentiates women's daily life experiences from those of men. Men and women may be affected differently by poverty because they "feel" it primarily through different channels, men as workers and women as consumers and reproducers. A gender-based division of labor may dictate special concern for certain kinds of issues based on the roles assigned to each gender (Kaplan 1982). Since women's identity and socialization are largely bound up with the private sphere, significant differences in the way men and women relate to and interpret the world are also likely to emerge (Sapiro 1983, 31). In fact, the creation of distinct gender identities may result in different psychological, cultural, political, and economic experiences for men and women (Sharistanian 1986b, 3). It may also have implications for their attitudes, including religious and political beliefs.

Family Roles and Poverty

Women in the CEBs display a remarkable degree of homogeneity in their roles, and these are, as Caldeira suggests, mainly defined in terms of family. The majority of women interviewed are both wives and mothers. Sixty percent are currently married and residing with their spouse.[22] Roughly another quarter are widows, with the remainder divided among never-married, divorced, and separated women. Thus, over 85 percent of the women interviewed have at some point in their lives been married. The exceptions include two young women in their early twenties, one of whom was "practically engaged" at the time of the interviews. Only one mature woman, Cíntia, in her mid-thirties, was never married and expressed no wish to marry.

All of the married and formerly married are also mothers. The size of their families ranges from two to thirteen children, with three to four children being typical.[23] Many of the older women, who no longer have school-age children at home, look after their grandchildren or neighbor children. While a few younger mothers with children under twelve participate, most CEB participants have at least one child old enough to watch the others, thus freeing them to attend meetings and so on.

Marriage and motherhood are important factors shaping women's lives. Both men and women are affected by these life changes, but Caldeira argues that they affect women more. Marriage and childbirth curtail women's extradomestic activities much more than those of men, reinforcing their essentially private identity (Caldeira 1984, 132–33). With marriage and the birth of a first child, women's lives become increasingly focused on the home and concentrated in the neighborhood.

As a *dona-de-casa*, or housewife, a woman is expected to spend her time in the home. And indeed, housework occupies an enormous amount of poor women's time (Caldeira 1984, 132). Women usually rise early in the morning to prepare breakfast and to pack lunches that the working members of the household will reheat at work. They spend most of the morning in a round of household chores, which are seemingly never done, or at least never to satisfaction. No matter how spotless a house is, the *dona-de-casa* will always apologize to a visitor for the state of confusion (*bagunça*). Children must also be taken

to school and perhaps fetched, often several times a day, because Brazilian schools operate several different sessions. A
hot lunch must be prepared, and dinner for all the workers,
who arrive at various times in the evening. The invariability of
women's schedules is apparent in the common scheduling
of CEB meetings: almost always in the afternoon, when they
can be squeezed in between housework and the preparation
of dinner.

Women's roles in the household rarely take them beyond
the neighborhood, except perhaps for occasional shopping or
to a health clinic or government office (Caldeira 1984, 125).
This lack of familiarity with the city beyond their neighborhood was expressed by Adelita. For her, participation in a base
community was a revelatory experience that literally expanded
her world:

> Being in the struggle, with the participation we have, is
> a beautiful thing. Even if we haven't had much chance to
> study, like me, myself, I don't know much. A person with-
> out schooling doesn't know much, not even how to get
> around, eh? And that was a very important thing. I, like I
> said, was a housewife. And look, now we go to every blessed
> place, trying, looking for things. (July 1986)

Women I interviewed would sometimes marvel that I had trav-
eled extensively in the parish and could find my way to meetings in CEBs they had never visited—without getting lost!

Their experience of the neighborhood and its problems is
in some respects more intense than that of men, whose work
often carries them to a distant part of town. Moreover, while
both men and women are affected by the problems of poor
neighborhoods, women are perhaps more greatly affected by
some through their role as primary caregiver for children.
Women, for example, are likely to take children to the community health post, if one exists, or to have to carry them to a

different part of town if one does not. They are familiar with the shortages of medicine, vaccines, personnel, and so on that limit their children's health care. They are more likely to be intimately familiar with the problems of schooling, since they see the children to school and back, past the garbage and drug dealers by the schoolyard fence.

Women are likely to feel and express their poverty through such problems. Similarly, their domestic roles mean that they see poverty in terms of consumption problems, such as an inability to provide sufficient food for their families. Much of women's group conversation in Itaim focuses on just such neighborhood and consumption problems. Women share their complaints, concerns, and information about prices and availability of items. During 1986, for example, many discussions in the CEB Mothers' Clubs included detailed information about where milk could be purchased in the neighborhood and about the practice of *ágio,* or charging above the government-fixed price for foodstuffs, at the local market (*feira*).

Employment: Unequally Shared Experience

In contrast to women's experiences in which daily life revolves around the neighborhood, home, and household reproductive tasks, men's role as breadwinner means that they generally spend little time at home. Particularly for blue-collar workers like the husbands of most of the women in the CEBs, work usually involves not only an exhausting day in a factory, but also lengthy commutes to and from work. Most work in the city or the industrial suburbs.

Itaim Paulista is linked to the distant city center by three types of transportation. The aging metropolitan rail system runs through Itaim proper. The old trains are dangerous, subject to breakdown, and crowded with people hanging out of doors and windows at rush hour. But in addition to convenience of location, they have the advantage of being the lowest priced means of reaching "the city."[24] For a higher fare, one can take the buses, which take about an hour to reach the last stop on the expanding east-west subway line.[25] The metro trip to the central metro stop at Sé, where many workers would change to another line, takes another half hour; and since there are never enough buses at rush hour, travelling to and from work each day can easily take four or more hours.[26]

One CEB member described her husband's commute to a factory: "My husband gets up before sunrise. He goes out in the sun, the rain, the cold, the heat. He goes to the station and gets a train that's already packed to go to work. He arrives in Tatuapé (station) and rides another train or bus, standing, for an hour and forty minutes to get to work" (Nov. 1986). Many residents who work in the city leave Itaim as early as five in the morning and do not return until eight in the evening. Buses, like the trains, are packed at rush hour, so many workers spend a good portion of their trip home standing squeezed into the aisle, or perhaps hanging out the back door. Older children may work in the city, spend the evening in night classes, and arrive home at ten or midnight, only to get up at five again the next morning. Moreover, Brazilians normally work a half-day on Saturday, so large amounts of commuting time are added to a work week that already exceeds forty hours.

Women certainly share in the world of work: 44 percent of the women interviewed had worked outside the home for pay in some capacity at some point in their lives, although only 37 percent did so while participating in the CEB. About a third of the women in the CEBs had worked in a factory-type situation at some point, the closest parallel to the typical blue-collar man's work experience, involving long and inflexible hours. Three worked in mixed male-female settings: a metalworks, electronics factory, textile mill. Most who described "factory work," however, had worked for some time in sewing sweatshops. Such work is not as well paid as regular factory work, and can involve longer hours. Cleide worked twelve hour days (6 A.M. to 6 P.M.) for six years (Aug. 1986). The regime in sweatshops is also quite rigid. Iraci recalled: "I worked there about fifteen years ago, but nothing has changed. There's a little plaque on the wall. You can be dying to go to the bathroom, but if that plaque doesn't say "free," you can't even get up from your machine" (Nov. 1986). She eventually left and went to work at Philco where she felt less "marginalized." Perhaps the single advantage of sweatshops is that they are scattered throughout the periphery, so women may be able to avoid the long commutes their husbands face.

Younger, unmarried women may prefer better-paid factory work to informal sector work. If educated, they also may have the option of quasi-professional work. The 37 percent of women working at the time of the interviews included a teacher, teacher's aide, day-care worker, and two office workers in church offices. Even with better earning potential, however, younger educated women will generally curtail their income when they have children. The one married mother of school-age children in this group, the public school teacher, worked only part-time in order to be home in the afternoon.

The need for flexible or part-time working hours, low skills, and work in the informal sector all lower women's earning capacity (Caldeira 1984, 85). Mothers of young children, especially, avoid full-time and inflexible work schedules because they often lack childcare alternatives. Work for a mother of young children is clearly a last resort, a fact that is reflected in statistics that show that the percentage of women in the labor force *increases* with the economic wealth of neighborhoods in São Paulo, while the participation of youths *decreases* (Caldeira 1984, 57).

When they must work, women often prefer sewing at home—an activity most of the women in the CEBs started when their children were young and continued at the time of

the interviews. In fact, if such work by women who call themselves "housewives" is included, nearly all of the women were
working when interviewed. The remainder of the women who
declared an occupation worked as maids or, in one case, as a
vendedora ambulante, selling used clothing door-to-door.

Like men, women working outside the home experience
poverty through exploitative work relations, through the individual experience of employment as well as through problems
of consumption and reproduction. However, it is also clear
that women and men share these experiences unevenly, with
the bulk of women's experience of poverty centering around
consumption and other "private sphere" issues, while men's
time and energy are taken up in extradomestic work, with less
direct experience of problems related to consumption, children's health and schooling, and so on.

Moreover, work outside the home apparently does little
to change women's essentially private identity. Caldeira states
that most wives and children who enter the work force perceive themselves and are perceived as auxiliary workers, who
are temporarily "helping" the primary, male earner. And indeed, given their lower earning opportunities, women's work
is subsidiary (Caldeira 1984, 92–93). Thus, both cultural expectations and marketplace realities combine to make most
women perceive the home as the source of their primary identity, and work outside the home as a temporary tactic—a burden, really—taken on to benefit the home and family unit.

Margarita exemplifies many working-class Brazilian women,
who view wage work largely in private terms. Her children told
her not to stoop to taking a janitor's job, but she says:

> Even if your mother didn't have much education, she was
> an important lesson in another way, making her children
> not be what she was, someone who worked at times at a
> job a little, well, lowly. The children won't have to do that.

Why? Because they have a mother and father interested in making them someone. The country doesn't need a family that is always poor, or without education. A mother has to think of her children. She goes to work, and in that way she can ensure the children's future for them. (Oct. 1986)

By working she was able to see that all of her children finished school and received some kind of further training. Margarita had one of the most extensive and varied work histories, having once been a metalworker, for example; but she defines herself primarily as a mother who worked on behalf of her children.

Even younger women with better labor market opportunities tend to share this view. Cristina, an educated professional in her thirties and the mother of two young children, also sees women's primary responsibility and identity in very private terms. Cristina described in very positive terms her own mother's complete availability to her eight children and contrasted it with what she sees as the breakdown of the family in contemporary Brazil. As a teacher, she blames the splintering of the family for many of her students' problems:

I don't know if that's why I think that the family is the basis of everything. All of [the students] with problems in the family—how that brings problems to school! They don't have their mother at home, the mother works all day because she is mother *and* father. Poor thing, she arrives home dead tired. She's just a walking shadow. She gets home, there's hardly time for dinner and bed. That's a child with a mother who's abandoned him. (Nov. 1986)

Marriage and children will most likely change the young women's work opportunities and may change their attitudes as well. For the majority of women in the CEBs, marriage and children have meant private sphere responsibilities and restricted labor market opportunities. While they may support in principle the notion that women have a right to work and to compete equally with men, few have any aspirations for enriching or fulfilling careers for themselves personally. When asked about hopes and aspirations for the future, only one woman aside from Cíntia, thirty-two year-old Simone, replied, "My dream is to have a terrific job" (Dec. 1986).[27] Changing the essentially private focus of their lives is neither an aspiration nor a realistic option for women with little education, few skills, and a family to raise. The daily realities of their lives and options, combined with cultural beliefs about women's appropriate roles, mean that most women in the CEBs derive their primary sense of identity from the private sphere, even if they often step outside it.

A Mother's Heart: Women's Special Gifts

In addition to mediating their perceptions of poverty and immediate material concerns, women's shared roles may also give them a larger, distinctive, and gendered way of viewing the world. Psychoanalytic feminists assert that women's private roles, particularly mothering, may give North American women a uniquely gendered perspective.[28] Carol Gilligan, for example, posits women's approach to justice as more contextualizing and relationship-oriented than men's legalistic reasoning, and relates the difference to women's greater immersion in the private sphere (Gilligan 1982). In a Latin American context, Renny Golden contends that Salvadoran women's patriotism differs from men's in its life-affirming emphasis on community and "the maintenance of social life" in the face of war and death (Golden 1991, 192).

These declarations have a great deal in common with *marianismo*'s emphasis on women's special gifts as nurturers, peacemakers, and the moral superiors of wayward, individualistic men. They all stress women's other-orientedness and capacity for nurturing family and community. Perhaps none of these attributes is truly a shared gender- or role-determined female characteristic. Nonetheless, it is important to realize that poor women in Brazilian CEBs do largely share a *belief* that women have special roles, gifts, and ways of seeing the world. They believe, further, that these are related to their ability to care for and nurture others, especially children.

The belief in women's unique perspective and gifts constitutes a shared referent for women in the CEBs. It is natural for them to speak in terms of caring, compassion, nurturing, and service to others: this is a women's language that engages them all. Its permeation of women's consciousness and ways of viewing the world can be seen in the persistence with which references to "a mother's heart," "women's special love," and concern for others continually emerge in the interviews. Such references pervade the interviews of all but the youngest, unmarried women.

Margarita, a fifty-five-year-old, illiterate grandmother, argued that women have more inner strength and a special approach to life:

> From a mother's heart comes everything for her son, for her daughter, for her son-in-law, for her grandchild, her siblings, her acquaintances. Not from a man . . . because man doesn't love. He loves, but his love is very different from yours. . . . Your love is greater than his. . . . That's why I say that woman has all the force to change the world to a new one, a better one. (Oct. 1986)

Thirty-two-year-old Simone, a mother of two who was studying computers at night school, eloquently expressed the belief that women bring a special vision to all they do. She described the reasons that women are organizing to help abandoned children: "At the bottom, the very bottom, it's for the children that we do everything. There are people who see all this and don't really see, don't understand. But we understand.

We see with the hearts of mothers. That's why women are in every fight. Not for themselves, but for all the people . . ." (Nov. 1986).

Two middle-aged women, Joselina and Iracema, expressed a similar belief in women's capacity to care for others, adding that this was a strong reason for their inclusion in political life. Joselina says that it would be good if more women candidates were elected to office because "women pay more attention to people, and give more attention to the poor" (Aug. 1986). Iracema's husband bitterly resents her activism in the CEB and one afternoon began criticizing her in a veiled way by saying that women should work in the shadows, like Mother Teresa, not in the limelight, like Margaret Thatcher.[29] Iracema's spirited defense revolved around the need for women to organize to change society, not to "bandage" problems. Women need to become involved in politics, she said, because they bring more love to it, and a maternal instinct. They think of *everyone's* children, and thus avoid the trap of individual competitiveness, thinking instead of the common good (field notes, Oct. 1986).

This shared emphasis on women's moral, other-oriented approach to life may reflect cultural models of *marianismo* as well as the real impact of women's roles and opportunities. When asked to describe Mary and the meaning of her model for women today, women in the CEBs often stressed her compassionate, caring nature, although they differed in the degree to which they perceived this compassion leading to action in the wider community. Margarita, for example, stressed Mary's examples of chastity, motherhood, and submissiveness. She portrayed her as a peacemaker in the family. If Mary gave an example of action in the wider world, it was one of discipleship within the church, according to Margarita (Oct. 1986). In a very similar, traditionally *marianista* description, Eloisa made one exemplary element of Mary's discipleship more concrete:

"She never stopped giving charity, doing good for others . . . and we too should help our brothers when they need us" (Oct. 1986).

Other women took the notion that women have a special capacity and responsibility for caring for others further, using the same basic images to posit a larger role for women as nurturers not just of families, but also of communities in ways that might exceed traditional face-to-face charity. Maria Angela described Mary's model as one of compassionate motherhood—really listening to and empathizing with one's children is extremely important to Maria Angela. In addition, she argues, Mary shows that women must be concerned with the well-being of others, as Mary was concerned "with the poverty of her time" (Nov. 1986). Similarly, Joselina and Iracema, who described women's special caring approach as a source of redemptive politics viewed Mary's model as one of nurturing in this larger sense. They see Mary as a woman of the people, like themselves, who has suffered as they do. Rather than being submissive, however, Mary struggled against poverty for the well-being of all (Aug., Apr. 1986).

A common perception of women's special gifts and roles, particularly a shared ability to love and care for children and those more generally in need unites the women in the CEBs as much as their actual, highly private-oriented roles and identities. Gender roles do shape the structure of daily life and almost certainly affect the ways in which individuals feel and react to poverty, and they may also ensure that women, with their "mothers' hearts," share a common ethic of care for children and those in need. Even if such an ethic is not gender-based, the perception of women's distinctive role is important. It gives the women in the CEBs a common language, a common sense of what is important and appropriate for them as women. They are not all more other-oriented than men; they interpret "caring" behavior in quite different ways. Nonetheless, they all uphold a standard for women's action that derives from their experiences in the private sphere and from cultural gender stereotypes. They share the belief that women should be and are uniquely disposed to care for and nurture others.

POVERTY, GENDER, AND RELIGION

Liberation theologians and liberationist pastoral agents have typically aimed their theology, pamphlets, and organizing at a social class: the poor. Yet poor men and women, despite their common experience of poverty, differ in their familial and social roles and the interests these dictate. Cultural expectations of their roles, behaviors, and values differ as well, and these cultural traditions are often strongly internalized by individuals, as the example of women's notion of a "mother's heart" suggests. Gender, then, may affect women's responses to new religious and political movements like the Popular Church in at least two ways. Their typical roles may shape their interests in ways that dictate a higher or lower level of participation or help determine the form of that participation.

Roles, socialization, and the internalization of values and attributes associated with gender may also give women a particular psychological or religious approach which shapes the degree to which they accept, reject, or reorient a liberationist message. The next chapter looks at the religious lives of women in the CEBs, and asks whether they share a gendered religiosity and how any shared characteristics influence their reception of a liberationist message.

FOUR

Each in Her Own Way

Gender and the Interpretation of Liberation Theology

CEBs at their height in the 1980s had a certain masculine aura. In Brazil, struggling under a military dictatorship, they were strongly identified with a new trade unionism born in the auto and steel factories, and with the political party it spawned, the leftist *Partido dos Trabalhadores* (PT). Unions in Brazil were historically created and controlled by the state, while populist party structures tended to be paternalistic, top-down mechanisms to secure the votes of the masses. Like the CEBs, the new unions and the PT defied traditional authoritarian structures, substituting a grassroots organizational style and a critique of Third World capitalism that resonated well with liberation theology. But the identification of these masculine movements with the CEBs was based on more than organizational and ideological affinity: well-known liberationists like Frei Betto and Cardinal Arns lent their legitimacy and their resources to the trade unions' famous strikes in the industrial suburbs of São Paulo. CEB activists played significant roles in the creation of both unions and the party. It was easy to imagine the CEBs in urban São Paulo full of militant factory workers and political activists.

In reality, the CEBs were more conventionally religious, less politicized, and more heavily female than their touted links suggested. As the dominance of Mothers' Clubs in group after group became apparent, so did the contrast with the male-oriented language, symbolism, and political stereotype of the groups. I decided to ask some pastoral workers how the preponderance of women affected the CEBs. Gender certainly makes a difference, a priest and sociologist who had studied the CEBs declared: women are so conservative and steeped in preconciliar church ways that all they want to do is pray, hindering the real work of the Popular Church. Of course gender makes a difference, a nun declared: women are more spiritual and community-oriented, they have greater inner strength and tenacity than men, and, despite the Popular Church's neglect of them, women have been its mainstay.

Both assumed that gender produces differences in religious attitudes and behaviors—in an individual's religious "personality." If so, then men's or women's predominance in a religious group could critically affect its outcome. Andrew Greeley explains: "The Church . . . is a complex and multifaceted phenomenon which emits many different signals. Which of the signals one chooses to focus on is . . . likely to be a function of one's own personality as a signal receiving mechanism" (Greeley and Durkin 1984, 16–17). For example, the church depicts God as father, judge, loving, all-powerful, and so on. Depending on religious personality, one person may focus on the image of God as a strict, enforcing judge, while another sees a kindly, comforting parent. If gender shapes that personality, a movement trying to emit a particular signal may find that either men or women are reinterpreting that signal to fit their own religious needs. Thus if women share a distinctive religious personality, it may be a key factor in their reception of the liberationist church's message of conscientization, a message developed by and sometimes seemingly aimed at men.

But just what effect does gender have in the CEBs? Does women's religiosity make them more radical or more conservative? Are they more likely than men to respond to the CEBs' religious message or to subvert it into traditional channels? Despite much agreement that gender matters, no one seems able to pinpoint its effect. Thus, we need to examine the assumption that women's religious personalities are gendered.

RELIGIOUS BEHAVIOR AND GENDER

Both the priest's and the nun's descriptions of "women's" religious personalities seem persuasive: Brazilian women's strong identification with the private sphere could lead logically to either description. As the bearers of religious tradition, women are probably an important channel of conservative, traditional religious authority. Familial concerns and piety may also lead them to the forefront of politically conservative religious movements, like the anticommunist marian societies of the 1950s, and the family-church-and-country marches that encouraged and legitimized the military coup of 1964 (Van den Hoogen 1990; Simões 1985). Greater reverence for religious authority might lead women to embrace new ideas presented by that authority more readily than men, however; and women's nurturing and care-giving roles and ethic certainly might form the basis for communitarian social action. Clearly, the same expressed values, concerns, and life experiences are capable of producing different outcomes. The only way to resolve the debate and to determine whether women's religiosity tends more in one direction or the other is to examine women's religious lives.

Conceptualizing religion as a factor explaining other—especially political—attitudes and actions is difficult. Social scientists have utilized denomination, measures of behavior such as frequency of attendance, and models of attitudes to try to capture the idea of "religion." All are important aspects of religion, but they tend to capture religion as a "socio-cultural phenomenon." We also need to take a more multi-faceted approach, including an examination of religious attitudes and values, to appreciate religion's "place in the personal life" (Allport 1973, 94).

Behavior—perhaps the most clearly gendered dimension of religion—is an important indicator of religion's "place in the personal life," especially in a country like Brazil where mass attendance and close affiliation with official church structures separate more orthodox Catholics from the many "popular Catholics." Popular or folk Catholics participate little and have very uncatechized religious beliefs; frequent mass attendees who perceive themselves as close to the church, in contrast, are more orthodox (Bruneau 1982, 42–43).[1] Liberation theologians have often implied that the CEBs reach unchurched, popular Catholics: rural dwellers and recent urban migrants with a simple folk faith.[2] The founding of the CEBs in Santo Antônio belies this claim.[3] While popular Catholics may be part of the large numbers of individuals who drift in and out of the CEBs to hear a mass or say a novena, the core group— those most likely to be affected by the liberationist message— are women who attend mass regularly and are close to the institutional church.

The single most common characteristic of the women in Santo Antônio is a shared history of long, intimate identification with the church. When asked to describe how they started in the CEB, most women echoed Marieta's statement: "I always knew," she said, "that I liked to go to mass" (interview, July 1986). Many, like Maria dos Anjos, connected church-going and family: "I liked it, I'm from a religious family, and we participated in the church, right? You know, just to go to mass and then go home again" (Oct. 1986).

Older women from the countryside shared Joselina's memories of overcoming difficulties to attend services: "We always went to mass, and we got up at the crack of dawn to go to mass . . . we got up and walked three hours, we went on foot, on the road, and in the middle of the brush, to go to mass and to confess. We waited in a line as long as the milk lines are nowadays!" (Aug. 1986).[4] Arriving in the newly-settled city periphery, many, like Fátima, continued to travel long distances if there was no parish nearby: "I'm from Minas, and we had that little life of always going to mass too . . . we had a church right nearby, we went to mass every Sunday. Then we moved here to Itaim, you know, to Robru, and we didn't have a church in the neighborhood. We went to mass in Guaianases."[5] Such memories usually evoked smiles of pride and pleasure.

Only five of the thirty women were not lifelong church attendees, and three of these remain occasional participants attracted more by the CEB's sociability and educational programs than its religious offerings. Two others, Gerci and Iraci, have become regular, practicing Catholics with their involvement in the CEBs. Gerci, a young woman from a nonpracticing family, literally grew up in the CEB, of which she became an integral member upon making her first communion at thirteen. Only Iraci is a lapsed Catholic. Yet Iraci's very reasons for lapsing express a strong attachment to the church: "I wasn't much of a one for church. I didn't like it, because I had this whole experience, I wanted to be a nun. Then came the second Vatican Council. The nuns stopped wearing habits, and then my father wouldn't let me be a nun. I kind of lost faith in the church. I didn't like it any more" (Nov. 1986).[6] Years later, when she came upon the CEB in her neighborhood, Iraci was reconciled with the church that had disappointed her youthful expectations. She is now an activist in the Workers' Pastoral, works at the diocesan office, and attends her CEB regularly.

Women in the CEBs typically have also been active in lay organizations. Women over fifty are likely to have taken on special roles in devotional practices and lay societies. Joselina always opened her home for devotions in May, the month of Mary: "I worked in the fields. I had the prayers for the month of Mary in my house—we really did it right. In May, we prayed all month at my house. As soon as I came from the fields, I got everything ready, and the priest came and led prayers for the month of May" (Aug. 1986). Other women were Daughters of Mary, or members of the Apostolate of the Sacred Heart, or the Legion of Mary. All of these organizations stress devotion, but also require their members to engage in charitable work.[7]

One younger woman, Cíntia, was active in the *Juventude Operária Católica,* a youth movement that was a precursor of the CEBs. Others are religious teachers: fully one-third of the women interviewed have been or are currently catechists or confirmation teachers. Three women traced their current participation back to their initial experiences as catechists.

Such ongoing involvement is a key to women's participation. In fact, nearly all the women attributed their initial involvement to an invitation from a priest or nun with whom they had a previous relationship through the parish. Joselina was recruited before she even moved to São Paulo:

> When I got here, I went to church, just to go to mass, see? So I went to [the CEB] Santa Rosa de Lima, went to mass and went home, and the next Sunday I went again. Then I think the priest suspected there were new people there, and asked where we were from . . . I said, "From Minas," and he said, "Ah, it's really you, your name is right here, you see?" I got scared, I said, "Why, my name?" And he said, "I have a letter here that the priest there sent, saying your family left the community there empty, that it's a family with the capacity to form a community." Then I felt so . . . I didn't know what to say, you know? (Aug. 1986)[8]

As noted earlier, intense, on-going participation in and identification with the church itself appears to be gendered. In a different part of São Paulo's periphery, Carmen Cinira Macedo confirms that women were slightly more likely than men to attend mass frequently and less likely not to attend at all (Macedo 1986, 114). Her findings probably *understate* the differences, because so few men were willing to respond to the survey. As she points out, "because the subject was religion, many men refused to speak, saying that women understand these things better" (Macedo 1986, III, translation mine). The few men who did respond (54 of 178 Catholics) were probably disproportionately likely to be those who felt comfortable with religion—and who attended mass more frequently.

Thus, the gap between men's and women's religious behavior manifest in women's higher participation in CEBs seems to be part of a wider gendered phenomenon in which women participate disproportionately in all religious activities. Women are disproportionately recruited for the CEBs because these draw on an audience of already-participating Catholics, and that audience itself is disproportionately female. If mass attendance and other behavioral indicators of religious orthodoxy are gendered, does it follow that these "orthodox" women share a common set of religious attitudes? Are their values and beliefs also gendered?

In fact, behaviors and attitudes are both important components of religious life, and can combine in a variety of ways.[9] The idea of "religious personalities," commonly occurring patterns of behavior-attitude combinations, can provide a means of dealing with the complex ways in which individuals live their religions. Several types of personalities exhibit orthodox behavior and yet have few values or attitudes in common. We need to know much more about women's inner religious lives, or religious personalities, before we can conclude that a gendered religiosity accounts for their response to the CEBs.

RELIGIOUS ATTITUDES, GENDER, AND LIBERATION THEOLOGY

Religious personalities are varied and complex, combining themes and attitudes in unique and often surprising ways.

Nonetheless, certain basic combinations of attitudes have been identified as different personality "types." Peter Benson and Dorothy Williams, in a North American study, identified six typical patterns or personalities (Benson and Williams 1982). Of these six, three—people-concerned, integrated, and self-concerned religionists—are associated with a high degree of church involvement and religious orthodoxy, the behaviors typical of CEB members (see table 1). While it might seem that one type of individual would reject the CEBs while another would become an active participant, it turns out that individuals of all three types are involved.

In fact, both the priest and the nun who described "women's" impact on the CEBs are right. Two of the religious personality types in the CEBs—self-concerned and people-concerned—fit their stereotypical descriptions of religious women. The third is a combination of the other two. Moreover, these personalities emerge in individual responses to the liberationist message, producing reinterpretation along conservative, pietistic lines, or embrace of its symbolism and political message.

The nun's description fits well with the personality described as "people-concerned." These individuals perceive religion as leading to interconnectedness with others; as a motive for adopting caring attitudes toward others; as "freeing and enabling" rather than disciplinary; and as a source of inspiration to action rather than comfort. Their most cherished value is social justice. In CEBs, these individuals respond readily to liberation theology and social mobilization. Hence, I prefer to call this group "liberationists," a more accurate and descriptive term in this context.[10]

In contrast, the priest's description of conventionally pious, conservative women dovetails neatly with a type that Benson and Williams call "self-concerned," but which I will call "traditional." Traditional religionists are more self- than community-oriented; perceive religion in terms of a personal

Table 1. Six Religious Types [a]

		Religionists				
	Legalistic	Self-Concerned	Integrated	People-Concerned	Non-Traditional	Nominal
Dominant Religious Themes [b]						
Agentic	1	1	1 or 2			
Communal			1 or 2	1	1	
Vertical		1	1 or 2	1	1	
Horizontal			1 or 2	1		
Comforting		1	1 or 2			
Challenging			1 or 2	1		
Restricting	1		1 or 2			
Releasing			1 or 2	1		1
Theological Orientation						
Christian Orthodoxy	1	1	1	2	3	3
Evangelical	2	1	2	2	3	3
Symbolic	2	3	3	3	1	1
Importance						
Pro-Church	2	1	1	2	3	3
Pro-Religion	2	1	1	1	2	3
Value Emphases	Self-restraint	Traditional values	Love	Justice	Justice	(Low on all)

[a] Adapted from Benson and Williams (1982): 124–125.
[b] High = 1; Moderate = 2; Low = 3

Table 2. Respondents by Religious Type [a]

Traditional[b]	Integrated	People-Concerned	Non-Traditional[c]	Nominal[d]
Clara	Carolina	Adelita	Catarina	Cleide
Conceição	Chica	Cíntia		Eliane
Eloisa	Cida	Gerci		Francisca
Margarita	Cristina	Iracema		
Marieta	Emilia	Iraci		
Neide	Fátima	Joselina		
Silvia	Marcela	M. dos Anjos		
	M. Angela	M. José		
	Marli	Simone		
		Zélia		

[a] There were no legalistic religionists in the sample.
[b] I substitute "traditional" religionists for Benson and Williams' "self-concerned" type.
[c] Value emphasis closest to people-concerned, grouped with them in interpretations of liberation theology.
[d] Similar to traditional with some integrated characteristics in interpretations of liberation theology.

relationship with God rather than a motive for caring for others; see it as a source of discipline, not as enabling; and as a source of solace rather than challenge. Their most cherished values are traditional ones, such as family and country (Benson and Williams 1982). While such people have a relatively self-regarding religious outlook, for Brazilian women, as we shall see, this type's traditional values came through much more clearly than the individualism, a fact that is not surprising given their culture, socialization, and roles.[11]

Finally, the third group, "integrated" religionists, mix themes from both of the other two. They see religion as comfort and challenge, as an individual relationship with God, a reason for caring for others, and so on. Their most clearly distinguishing feature is a value emphasis on love: face-to-face Christian caring is their preference, in contrast to the people-concerned religionists' emphasis on social justice. Because the label "integrated" is not descriptive, I prefer to refer to this group as "samaritans," in order to highlight their value emphasis.[12]

The active CEB members interviewed were almost evenly divided among the three types.[13] Seven women were traditional; nine, samaritans; and ten, liberationists (see table 2). If we add the infrequent participants to the traditional category, where their interpretation of liberation theology seems to fit best, then traditional and liberationist religionists have equal levels of participation. The numbers in this sample are too small to discuss percentages or to be generalized, but the surprising failure of any one group to dominate the CEBs is notable.

This mix of religious personalities within the CEBs, however, does not seem unique to Santo Antônio. In his study outside Rio de Janeiro, John Burdick identified a number of very similar religious types. Two groups—one with a strong attachment to preconciliar values and one with an emphasis on charity—are quite similar to what I call traditional religionists. Another, which mixes charity with a more postconciliar Catholicism, is quite similar to the samaritans described here (Burdick 1993, 185–89). Differences in religious styles and personalities among those recruited, not gender, account for the minority of members who actively embraced consciousness-raising and liberationist ideas.

The Liberationist Minority

The liberationist message is a complex one that mixes spirituality and politics in its religious symbolism. Nonetheless, for purposes of understanding the church's role in political and social change, it is important to understand how and whether individuals have responded to liberation theology's explicitly political message. Do they share its idea that sin is not individual but social, and structured into a capitalist economic system? Do they agree that Christ's message is for the political and economic liberation of the materially and political marginalized? Do they believe that at least some aspects of the kingdom of Heaven are realizable now, on earth, through political means such as the creation of socialism? Liberation theology cannot be reduced to these messages, but neither can it be said that an individual who does not share these ideas shares the "consciousness"—or the political project—of the Popular Church.

Nearly everything about a liberationist religious personality suggests an affinity to the Popular Church. Their communal orientation, view of religion as a challenge to action, and social justice orientation all fit with liberation theology's class-based, religio-political themes. Moreover, they are less strongly pro-church than some types, such as traditional religionists. This might allow them to accept some liberationist criticisms of the traditional church hierarchy more readily. Similarly, liberationists consciously examine and reevaluate religious beliefs, a characteristic that may incline them toward consciousness-raising and the reinterpretation of religious symbols along liberationist lines.

Liberationist women in the CEBs share the hallmarks of a communal approach, challenge orientation, and social justice values. And they are the most disposed to accept liberation theology; in fact, they alone clearly articulate liberationist sentiments. Their descriptions of liberationist symbols—almost always classic restatements of the major liberationist themes— show their commitment to social justice and willingness to link their religious convictions to political activism.

Iracema and Iraci are typical liberationists. Individuals with a communal approach to religion "relate their religion strongly to being connected with and responsible for other people. . . . The path to salvation comes through exercising caring and compassion for other people, doing good for others" (Benson and Williams 1982, 111-12). Liberationist women tend to express this communal approach through the idea of caring and service as their religious vocation. Iracema says that the desire to serve "is in our blood" (Apr. 1986). Iraci referred to the integral role that service has in her life:

> Sometimes I'm talking to my husband and I say, look, if I had been *conscientizada* before, I wouldn't have gotten married. You know? Because I think that marriage is such a little thing, with all the other things there are out there! . . . despite all the liberty I have, participation, conversation and all, I think I still give very little of myself. I think I have much more to give, but I don't have the means. I'm married, I have children, I have to stay home and all. But I think my heart's too big to do so little for others. (Nov. 1986)

As a young girl, Iraci wanted to be a nun, although her father forbade this. Her desire could plausibly be linked to an ideal of service rather than retirement from the world.

Maria dos Anjos's father limited her participation in service activities; but she added happily, "When I got married, thank God, my husband and I, we are two people who live for the people, not for ourselves. We live for others. So when he comes home and finds me here, he says, hey, what are you doing here? He knows that my life is really out there in the street" (Oct. 1986). She also stressed the importance of the CEB as a community, as "a brotherhood" that helps its members:

> It seems to me, Carolina, that a woman who lives in the street, I'm sure that God helps her in many ways. She is making the future of all the people, and that is what God wants. She is living the gospel, because those in the struggle are always evangelized. Then, through the struggles, it's not that we're content with what we earn, but it seems we always have enough to share. And when we don't, some help always comes from somewhere. It is a brotherhood. Someone helps me, and I help. We live that way. (Oct. 1986)

The ideal of community that lies behind the larger struggles in which they participate is also something liberationists live from day to day in the CEB.

Liberationist religionists couple this sense of community and service with a view of religion as a challenge (Benson and Williams 1982, 130).[14] They often felt "called" or responsible for the emerging communities. Iracema said she "felt a weight fall on [her] shoulders" when the priest said in a sermon that people needed to participate more. She promptly went out and joined a women's group within the CEB (Apr. 1986). Iraci expressed the "call" she feels differently:

> In the community a girl . . . said once, "I'm poor because God made that choice for me. I didn't choose to be poor. But with lots of strength I'll respond to his challenge." I thought that was very beautiful. I think that's just exactly right. I'm poor, and I'll struggle to change that. Making an option for the poor isn't being poor, too. No, it's leading to changes for the poor. (Nov. 1986).

As a young mother of seven sons, Zélia longed for the time when she could participate outside her home:

> I used to say to my neighbor, I can't wait to see them grown. Because after they've grown, they won't need me any more, and when something important comes along, I'll really go! . . . And when this business of the CEBs came along, it captivated me so much . . . and that's when all the fights started at home. . . . Then we really had some con- flicts, my God! How many times I fought, I argued, I even went on the sly! (Oct. 1986)

Like Gerci, for whom the CEBs have become "my life's proj- ect," Zélia responded to the challenge and opportunity of the CEBs with total commitment (Oct. 1986).

Prayer remains important to these women, but not only as petition or consolation. Iracema says they "continue to pray, because that is [their] force." But as another woman commented: "Today we pray because that is our strength, but we see that the role of women is not just to pray. . . . Also we learned that it's no good to keep praying every Sunday and not go out to the struggle. . . ."[15] Prayer becomes a source of strength that enables them to respond actively to what they perceive as God's challenge to Christians in a poor country.

An ability to critique earlier patterns of religious behavior, as well as church institutions, is indispensable to this group's embrace of liberation theology. Only three of these women—Gerci, Cíntia, and Simone—were raised in the post-Vatican II church; the rest were in their fifties or sixties in 1986. They were raised in traditional parishes with Latin masses and prayers to the saints for miracles. The Popular Church was sometimes in conflict with the official hierarchy and opened uncharted territory for them. The ability to criticize the church itself and their own prior religious behavior probably helped them to make the transition.

Liberationists are less "pro-church" than traditional religionists. They separate church and religious faith and may criticize the church as sometimes inhibiting the mature exercise of religious faith. Liberationist women often criticized specific actions taken by the hierarchy which they perceived as being aimed at reining in the CEBs to conform to a more sacramentally-oriented model of the church. They correspondingly place a great emphasis on *conscientização* as the mission of the CEBs, because "conscientized" faith is mature faith.

Cíntia, for example, complained that the church hierarchy was trying to restrict CEB members to strictly religious, rather than political, activities:

> Why should I go [to church council meetings] and lock myself up there to talk about nothing when there is important work to be done? The church can't live closed off— my political work is important, and it is linked to my faith,

but I can't live just in the church. . . . If it's just to go to
those council meetings, I tell you sincerely, I won't go. (field
notes, Dec. 1986)

Gerci, the young sector coordinator, also criticizes the church
for hindering conscientized people from acting on their faith in
the world through political organizations (Oct. 1986).

Zélia also believes that the church is now undermining the
CEBs, and wondered aloud why this should be so:

> You've perceived this, because you're participating. You've
> seen. And I've talked about this with Sister Cecilia. I just
> don't know what's happening, whether it's the fear of the
> "big people" in the church, the cardinals, the pope and that
> whole gang. They're afraid that if these communities start
> to wake up, something could come about. . . . The people
> could start fighting for their rights. Could that be what
> they're afraid of? (Oct. 1986)

Later she added that she will stop participating if the CEB and
Clube de Mães revert to more traditional religious activities.

Iracema echoed the conviction that at "certain levels," and
on certain issues, the church "seems to close. We don't have
space in the church" (Apr. 1986). But she made a distinction,
"I would never be able to leave this work in the community,
because once you start, this work never stops, and there's no
one else to take it over. Now, we don't want to see this work
die. That's why I'll never abandon the community. But the
sector, the diocese—I'll leave that" (Nov. 1986). Like Iracema,
most of the women combined criticism of the institutional
church with a high degree of commitment to their own communities.[16]

One reason these women are so committed to their communities is their embrace of consciousness-raising, a fact that
further marks them as liberationist religionists. A tendency to

re-examine religious beliefs is unusual, a hallmark of people-concerned religionists generally and liberationists in the CEBs. Despite the Popular Church's commitment to consciousness-raising, most people simply dislike it. Only about half of all CEB members participate in reflection (Hewitt 1985, 136). Leaders like Joselina realize this:

> We can't form a community through politics, or even through the Bible, not even the Bible can form a community. It has to be to pray the rosary at home. The people like to pray the rosary! [Laughter] . . . they don't understand the Bible either. If we pray the rosary, everybody likes it, everybody knows it, see? So that helps. (Aug. 1986)[17]

One nun said regretfully that women in a literacy group resented the time taken from their studies when she proposed a Bible reflection (field notes, Aug. 1986).[18] Similarly, I witnessed on several occasions the general discontent that broke out when a nun insisted on stopping for "reflection" at the end of a CEB-run sewing class. Fifteen minutes before the end of class when the women saw the nun going for her Bible, many would automatically begin to say, "Ah, sister, I have to go home now and prepare the meal" (field notes, May, Aug. 1986).

In contrast, liberationists all describe the excitement they felt about reflecting on the Gospels as a key to their CEB experience. Gerci remembers:

> Then I started in catechism class. And I was getting very interested in it, despite the fact that the catechist still used the old traditional method. What I liked best was when . . . we reflected on the gospel. I don't even know why or how. I picked up the gospel. [The catechist] said it was important for us always to put the gospel in our lives. . . . Then I started to reflect on this, and I put my ideas to the group.

So I was leading the reflection for the group . . . every
Monday. . . . And you know, I was really enjoying it. . . .
(Oct. 1986)

Others have gone on to Bible study groups and even a "popular" theology course and cite particular instances of reflection
as a key to their later participation in the CEB.[19] Their tendency to question and rethink their religious beliefs reinforces
the challenge dimension of the liberationist women's personalities.

Finally, liberationists' descriptions of symbols fit well with
a value emphasis on social justice, also characteristic of this type
of individual. They constitute the minority of CEB members
who believe that Christ's message is one of material and political liberation, that the social sin of capitalism is the font of
much of what has traditionally been called individual sin, and
that God's kingdom is partially realizable on earth through political and social justice. Their statements on these themes are
as classic and articulate as those of many theologians.

Zélia spontaneously gave her view of Christ's example.
Describing a strike and the conditions that the workers were
struggling against, she said:

I perceive very clearly that, when we go and look at Christ,
that isn't what he wanted. Christ, he died, he came to fight
against all that. And now we have to ask ourselves what we
will do. I think we have to fight, too. That's my thinking.
That alienated religion that just sits there, that isn't being
the Church of Jesus Christ. (Oct. 1986)

Iracema led a Sunday celebration that emphasized the unity of
the people, led by Christ in the struggle for earthly justice.
Concerned that the parish rejected the theme "faith and politics" as a diocesan priority, in favor of the topic of children,
she said: "I just can't understand it. For me, faith and politics

are inseparable." One can't, she argues, spiritually approach the problem of abandoned children without fighting the social conditions that cause abandonment (field notes, Oct., Nov. 1986).

Maria dos Anjos laughed when I mentioned that someone told me that Christ came to liberate people from their sins. She described Exodus in classic liberationist terms, saying that God intervened in history to lead his people out from under the yoke of oppression. Moreover, Christ's mission was to show us the way to fight for liberation, especially liberation from poverty and exploitation. Equality, she said, begins in the here-and-now, not after death (Oct. 1986).

These statements suggest acceptance not only of the idea of Christ as a liberator from poverty, but also of the unity of temporal and spiritual history. The women see themselves working to advance history toward the fulfillment of God's plan. They identify that plan with the elimination of sinful social structures, especially capitalism, that cause poverty and dehumanize the poor.

Capitalism was even held to be the cause of death of a young man shot in a drug-related incident. Described as a "victim of the violence of an oppressor system, fallen in the flower of youth," his death was equated with those of children victimized by poverty. Cíntia had no doubt where the "social sin" lay and how to respond to it: "We're not going to wait for God to do something. We are God. God is us. We have to act. Miracles don't fall from the sky. We have to end the violence of the capitalist system" (field notes, Nov. 1986). Iraci and Maria dos Anjos described capitalism as the "desert" from which people must free themselves with God's help (Oct., Nov. 1986). Zélia said that in order to achieve the new, just society to which they aspire, what must change is simply "The whole system, the system of the country, capitalism. . . . People want to be capitalists, but capitalism is what causes these injustices . . ." (Oct. 1986). Maria dos Anjos deepened this analysis by connecting social and personal sin. The exploitation of the workers produces misery, problems in the family, alcoholism, and other evils, such as crime. Thus most individual sin is "social" in origin, and will be overlooked by God. In contrast, he will not forgive those who are behind the exploitative system itself and who go unpunished by it now (interview and field notes, Oct. 1986).

The liberationist religionists are also certain that working to overturn unjust social structures means creating socialism, although its content is not always well-defined. To Maria dos Anjos, it meant simply that "the workers should move up three or four degrees."[20] Iraci admitted her confusion about the term, but added:

> But in my mind, I still think of the kingdom of God, you know? I think that it's where people have food, land, houses, a good salary, you know? I believe a lot in a society like that, where we have everything, and everybody has everything . . . but it's not clear to me what type of socialism. I see that as a Christian, as children of God, we should have abundant life, all good things. (Nov. 1986)

Iracema said that Brazilians in the CEBs want a sort of communism—a Christian communism that brings well-being, a sharing of goods, and more participation for all. That is the new society, the promised land. Such socialism would not follow a European model, however; it would respect the Catholicism of the Brazilian people and be created with "love" and "caring" (field notes, Sept. 1986).

Despite confusion about how socialism would look, only liberationist women share the liberation theologian's equation of "socialism" with the kingdom of God. Zélia began by saying: "To really have equality, that would be socialism, a type of socialism. . . . We who study the Bible, we see that the society Christ wanted was that kind. . . . Socialist" (Nov. 1986). Catarina was discussing her belief in the desirability of a socialist transformation when I asked what she meant by socialism. "The kingdom of God," she answered, "what Christ preached" (Sept. 1986).

These views on Christ's liberating message, sin and salvation, and the realization of the kingdom come closer to the spirit of liberation theology than those of any other group within the CEB. Liberationists respond to the challenge of liberation theology and embrace it wholeheartedly. They accept its political dimensions, and take up the task of combining religion and politics in a way that they hope will transform society and improve the lives of the poor. Much more surprising is the continued presence in the CEBs of a significant group of women whose religious personality leads them to an almost outright rejection of liberation theology: the traditional religionists.

Traditional Women: Staying Despite Dissonance

When pastoral workers set out to form new CEBs, they often recruit people who already attend the parish church and who are catechists or active in lay organizations. While some of those individuals have traits that mark them as liberationist religionists, many others' religious lives and needs are very different. Traditional religionists are even more strongly attached to the institutional church than their liberationist peers; however, they look to the church primarily for comfort, moral guidance, and personal salvation. Theirs is an inward-oriented religiosity that values a vertical relationship with God over an outward-looking, horizontal relationship with others.

This personality seems to be at odds with the CEB ethos, yet ten of the thirty women interviewed were traditional religionists—almost as many as were liberationists (see table 2). Most are older women, who were socialized in the church prior to Vatican II. Many of the former apostolate members fall into this category. Burdick highlights their socialization and prominence in pre-CEB church organizations in characterizing a similar group in his study, but it is important to recognize that many liberationist women share these characteristics as well (Burdick 1993, 188).

Margarita exemplifies this type of CEB member. Fifty-five years old and from Minas Gerais, a state known for its religious traditionalism, Margarita has participated in many devotional societies, including Daughters of Mary. Only her illiteracy prevented her from participating more fully. For her, religion—whether in the traditional parish or the CEB—is primarily a source of comfort. Her own difficult life (an abusive and often absent husband, in addition to material poverty) suffuses her description of religion's importance to her:

> Ah, it seems you forget all the problems you left behind! In our lives, so many things happen. There are women who leave the house beaten by their husbands, and go to church to see God. To see Him truly, in His Word, with faith, seeing Him before us. . . . We see Him like a child does, as a great man with open arms, we can see Him seated in a garden, or as a child playing. . . . Then a woman who left home desperate, beaten, pushed, her children in the brush where she took them so the husband wouldn't kill them, she arrives in church, you speak of God, she begins to see. "Here I've found peace, I've found solace, a place where I can hide my children. I'll hide them here in God." (Oct. 1986)

The importance of comfort in her religious orientation is also reflected in her statement that faith is a source of courage, in combination with the absence of challenge or social justice themes in her statements (Benson and Williams 1982, 118).

Traditional religionists also stress religion as discipline, commenting often on personal morality and issues like virginity. Margarita spoke at length about the importance of virginity for unmarried women. She commented that "Young people today have no morals, and neither do the old." And she repeatedly returned to Christ's command, "Go and sin no more" (Oct. 1986). Other traditional religionists, like Neide, also spoke frequently of the immorality of local youths, and the need for moral rectitude (Sept. 1986).

The implicit emphasis on individual rectitude and salvation contrasts strongly with the liberationist women's views and becomes even clearer in the traditional religionists' interpretation of themes in liberation theology. Traditional women quite simply reject the symbol of Christ as a liberator from material want. Margarita agreed that there is such a thing as political liberation, but "When it's time for church, it's liberation with Christ" that is at issue. Her interpretation is unambiguous and diametrically opposed to Iracema's:

> Let's not mix politics with the church. Because if we're talking politics, it's about rights. "Ah, Jesus worked that way, it's in the Bible . . ." No! That's not written there, church and politics, no. "Ah, but Jesus died for . . ." No! Jesus died for the salvation of sinners! He died for all of us. We're all sinners. So our work with Jesus, it's a different way to liberation of the people. (Oct. 1986)

Later she made the point even more clearly: "My way of asking that Jesus convert his people ever more in His name, is in the liberation of, how would you say, of faith, of morals. . . . If we lose morality, our faith, we are demoralizing Jesus. We are crucifying Him again even worse than in those days" (Oct. 1986). She went on to say that a "liberated woman" is one who is close to Jesus, and who as a result can liberate men—that is, keep them from falling into sin.

Cristina, thirty-six years old, criticizes the "error" of interpreting Christ as liberator of the "poor":

For lots of people, for the majority of people, and especially those who work in the community, when they say poor, for them, it's poor in money. It's like I said, they curse the rich. So they take it very literally. Because I think that the word "poor" is much broader than only not having money. You can be poor, and be very rich, as I see it. You can have no money at all, but you have a great Christian life. Then you're rich. And if you're not poor, but don't know Christ, well, then, you're really, truly poor. (Nov. 1986)

She concluded by saying that many people in the pastoral groups get all mixed up because of politics, and pass on "incorrect," politicized ideas to the people:

So the vision of liberation, liberation I think is open to everyone. Poor and rich, with and without money, even with a hard heart, eh? So the people really confuse spiritual and material poverty. The rich person never really has a chance to be saved. I think that's wrong. I give just as much chance to be saved to [a rich Brazilian politician] as to Saint Augustine! (Nov. 1986)

In contrast with liberationist women who reject traditional church symbolism, traditional women reject the new liberationist ideas as individual "mistakes" and not a "real" part of the church.

Traditional religionists quite simply reinterpret liberationist themes to fit with their own religious perspective. As Burdick notes, they "learned to recite with varying degrees of consistency the rights-oriented version of liberation yet privately continued to adhere to pre-comunidade understandings" (Burdick 1993, 188). Just as they substitute "liberation" for the more traditional "salvation" in their lexicon, so they continue to see all sin as personal rather than structural. They may agree that conditions in Brazil are unjust, but they attribute injustice to the malice of individuals rather than to the structure of capitalism. Neide thinks that *os grandes*, the "big people," are particularly hard-hearted and try to squeeze workers to make more profits. But she sees this as an individual characteristic, quickly pointing out that poor people also exploit each other all the time (field notes, Sept. 1986). Similarly, Cristina describes the source of Brazil's problems as *ganância*—greed. But, she adds, the poor are as greedy as the rich and contribute their share to the problems (Nov. 1986).

The traditional religionists' interpretation of the kingdom of God and how it will be achieved also conforms to their more comfort- and spiritual-orientation. While they agree with liberation theology that God desires a better life and an end to suffering on earth for all, they see this as a utopia that, even if achieved, would not constitute the kingdom of God per se. Margarita, for example, described her desire to "live the kingdom of Heaven" by living spiritually, alone, drawing on an inner strength (Oct. 1986). Traditional women insist upon a strong spiritual element in the kingdom of God that is much weakened in the liberationist interpretation.

Perhaps for that reason, traditional religionists are also likely to see the kingdom as attainable not through politics, but through personal conversion alone. They definitively reject the equation of socialism and the kingdom. Neide is particularly adamant in rejecting communism. She criticizes people in the CEB for thinking communism will solve their problems because it will give them something to eat. It will also, she says, break up families, force women to work, and undermine religion. This cannot be what God wants.[21]

Cristina describes the "new society" of the CEBs as one of sharing and brotherhood in which poverty would be eliminated. But she does not believe that socialism would be a step

toward that reality. In fact, she denies that any political or economic system will help to achieve her utopia. Instead, she says,
it must be personal:

> You know, we bring up things about socialism, commu-
> nism, capitalism. . . . But I think Christianity would be
> enough . . . I think we have to follow that single example,
> Christ. That's why I told you it's a great utopia, because
> it is very personal. You can maybe do it, but until the ma-
> jority of people are able to live that way, it's really a utopia.
> (Oct. 1986)

Rather than a political movement, she adds, what is required
is to work for the conversion of each person, especially the
young:

> Changing the child, then this child becomes an adolescent,
> and the adolescent an adult—I'm changing the society, am
> I not? It's not necessary to make a big movement. I think
> it's small changes that are needed. We have the example of
> Christ. He didn't create a big movement. We always say he
> did little things . . . a word, a gesture, no? (Oct. 1986)

According to traditional religionists, this kind of personal conversion could facilitate cooperation between capitalists and
workers so that capitalism would not have to be eliminated to
bring it more in line with God's plan. In fact, these women are
adamant that private property is a right to be respected, and
that capitalists have rights to their income. If hearts were converted, capitalists and workers could join together to help each
other and all would prosper.[22]

These interpretations of liberationist themes clearly reflect
the traditional women's religious emphasis on personal morality and an individual relationship with God. This places
them quite close to the highly individualistic, politically conservative category of "self-concerned religionists" that Benson

and Williams identified in their study in the United Sates. But the women in this category are not as strongly self-regarding as Benson and Williams's "self-concerned religionists." In fact, the rationale for calling them "traditional" rather than "self-concerned" derives from the fact that the latter connotes a degree of individualism that is notably absent among all these respondents. They do emphasize the personal, comforting aspects of religion and stress individual rectitude and personal salvation. Their value emphasis, like that of "self-concerned religionists," is on "traditional values" such as home and family. For Brazilian women, however, these values themselves require a certain degree of other-orientedness.

Despite their relative individualism, these women were formed by a church and society that stressed the proper role of women as selfless sacrificers on behalf of others, particularly their families. Their religious background also includes participation in groups that encouraged the idea that good Christians—and good women—cared for the poor in their communities. In recalling their pre-CEB experiences, many traditional women recollected their charitable works. In this sense, they most closely resemble Burdick's preconciliar Catholics, who "interpret 'liberation' . . . as a reminder to give charity and to seek other-worldly salvation" (Burdick 1993, 185). Eloisa described in great detail and with great affection her charitable work in the Legion of Mary in her hometown of Ilhéus in the northeastern state of Bahia (Oct. 1986). Neide, a member of the apostolate, recalled that they undertook various charitable activities, including "taking food to the needy" (Sept. 1986).

Traditional women like Margarita are in many ways the polar opposite of liberationists like Iracema. Liberationist women and pastoral agents recognize that traditional women do not share liberationist views even when they use words like "liberator." In fact, Iracema and Zélia often discouraged me from interviewing women like Margarita in their groups, saying that they simply "don't understand" what the CEBs are "really" about.

Despite the apparent potential cognitive and personal conflicts for traditional women in the CEBs, they remain an important presence, as their numbers among the most active women in the groups attest. Two traits that they share with liberationist women probably account for this continued presence. First, their strong personal identification and long history with the Catholic Church may encourage them to overlook any "discrepancies" in the CEBs, as Cristina's testimony suggests. Second, the value they place on service and charity and the connection these have for them with church groups make at least some of the activities of the CEB appealing to them. While their definition of service and its equation with charity rather than structural change place them at odds with liberationist leaders, it remains possible for the two groups to find common ground.

Samaritans: Combining Charity and Justice

The remaining women active within the CEBs are samaritan religionists, a group whose religious personality places them between the individualist and communitarian extremes of traditional and liberationist women. This group combines the sentiments of the other two almost equally: it is composed of women who respond to themes of both individualism and community, who see religion as a vertical relation to God and a horizontal one to one's fellow creatures as both a comfort and a challenge. Moreover, their value emphasis—love—can be construed as an intermediate position between the traditionalists' notion of charity and the liberationists' commitment to social justice.

In some respects it is difficult to identify samaritan religionists because they share with all of the respondents a concern for the less fortunate, for children, and for helping. But although all respondents express themselves in similar terms, the samaritan religionist group is distinguished from the traditional women by their greater tendency to see crime and poverty as socially caused. They are much less ready to condemn individuals for laziness or sinfulness. Yet they are different from the liberationist religionists because they do not share the analysis of capitalism as a system which is sinful, and do not see political solutions as paramount. Like Burdick's CEB members who equated liberation with self-reliance, this group sees liberation as a call to help others worse off than themselves (Burdick 1993, 186).

The "middle ground" on which they stand becomes clear in the women's discussion of the question of social sin. This group shares with the first the strong conviction that crime and marginality are the products of a sinful social reality, and that we should turn to the victims of that reality, even criminals, with love. This view alone puts them quite at odds with many people outside the CEBs and with the more traditional women.

Chica expresses this analysis when she says that things must be changed in Brazil so that all children and mothers have enough food, health care, and so on. Then children will not be abandoned to grow up as criminals in the streets: "It's very sad, isn't it? That shouldn't happen. Because God put us all in the world, all pure. But society is what spoiled all that" (Dec. 1986). Maria Angela also shares the conviction that "badness is born from misery." Those who steal and assault do so from hunger, and cannot be condemned (Nov. 1986). She referred to her own difficult experiences as a recent migrant from Minas Gerais, and said she was sometimes pushed to the brink of stealing to feed her two children, particularly after her husband's internment in a mental hospital.

But the samaritans are less clear that social sin is structured into a capitalist socioeconomic system. Instead, they tend to be closer to the traditional women's view that the deplorable aspects of society are a result of individual human activity. For example, Maria Angela cited the fact that, although she could understand how others fall into temptation like theft, she herself did not, in part because of the support of friends. Consequently, they are much less clear that a change in political system would be a step toward the reign of justice on earth.

Maria Angela began by describing the kingdom of God in rather ambiguous terms:

> To learn to live in union with people. That unity that we talk about becomes the kingdom of God, no? . . . kingdom of God is there in the highest heaven, but He must reign. When we pray the Our Father, we are asking for that kingdom here on earth. . . . for that kingdom really to be within us, I would have to give much more of myself to extend the kingdom here, understand? (Nov. 1986)

It soon became apparent, however, that the kingdom of God meant primarily living in community with others. For her it includes many particular types of acts:

> We go to help our brother in his needs, his problems. . . . And if we act that way, we are going more into the kingdom of God here on earth. . . . I should listen to you, because you have problems and I do, and listening is what is lacking. Many times that is missing among us, the kingdom. For us to listen to people, also to give when necessary, that also is part of the kingdom of God. (Nov. 1986)

Maria Angela also stressed "true charity" which she defined as giving not just what we have that is superfluous but "taking things from our use" to give food or clothing to others.[23]

But while this description is in most respects quite traditional, Maria Angela does share the conviction that religion involves active participation to help others, not just sacramental devotion. And she, in contrast to the traditional women, believes that politics, not just charity, plays at least some role in moving toward the kingdom because it can improve the lives of the poor:

> O yes, politics has to do with the kingdom of God. . . . Why should we choose the PT? Because it is on the side of the poor, it can do something for us. Politics also has to do with that. . . . Isn't the church on the side of the poor? Well, then, in politics too, we must choose a politics that works in favor of the church, in favor of the poor. (Nov. 1986)

Other women expressed more strongly the conviction that faith is related to politics. Chica, for example, believes rather traditionally that the poor are rich with God—a position she shares with Cristina. She describes her vision of a good society as one in which the "rich help the poor" by giving to them out of charity. But she also believes that politics is linked to faith, and that this is part of Christ's example:

> Some people think that in church one shouldn't talk about politics. Politics is one thing and religion is another . . . but every injustice we fight against, that's politics, isn't it? And Jesus talked about that, that injustice shouldn't be, and they killed him. . . . He fought against injustice, and that's politics, too. (Dec. 1986)

In a similar vein, Marli says:

> the gospel is very political, people! Jesus was political. People don't know that. Why was he political? He was political, he led a political life. He died because he wanted one thing, and the kings wanted another. . . . But the people don't understand that. . . . It's faith and politics, and faith has politics. Without faith, no one can do anything. Also without politics. (Nov. 1986)

Even when they express a conviction that politics is important, though, this group of women is unlikely to equate socialism with liberation. Rather, they emphasize conversion and reform. Chica and Maria Angela, for example, do not believe that capitalism is the problem. Rather, it is the hard hearts and greed of particular capitalists. To overcome that requires a mixture of prayer and politics. The rich must be "converted" to a willingness to share more with the poor, but at the same time laws could help to spread the wealth more equitably (Nov., Dec. 1986). Similarly, Marli says that they do not need to end capitalism, but rather to make new, more equitable laws. That way all would be equal not in terms of income, but in terms of the respect and treatment they receive (Nov. 1986).

Marcela shares the conviction that capitalism should not be condemned out of hand. Rather, like Cristina, she believes that individual greed is the problem. In order to combat that, she says, it is "necessary to change yourself first" to a more Christian attitude. Then, you must also conscientize people and organize them to demand their rights (Nov. 1986).

This mixture of liberationist and more traditional interpretations is also clear in Marcela's description of the significance of Christ as liberator:

> Some say that he wasn't holy, that he was more like a Tiradentes, that he was political and all. There are people who say that. I judge that he was a little bit holy, and a little bit political. Because what he did was also politics. He confronted the Hebrews, the Levites, he went to the temple. . . . As he did all that, he was against that whole system. . . . They say he was subversive. I don't know. Whether he was political—he was.[24]

Asked whether Christ's project was one of liberating the poor, she replied:

> Poor of money? No. He saw the poor of spirit, not of money. I don't have money, not that much money, but I

am rich. . . . He came to say, look, everybody is equal. So there's no poor, and no rich. . . . He didn't come to liberate the poor. He came for us to open our eyes, and see that everyone is equal. (Nov. 1986)

This means, she explained, that we should all love each other and get along, even Brazil and the United States.

In sum, the samaritan religionists share certain aspects of the liberationist interpretation. They believe that social conditions cause sin, for example, and that Jesus' example is political as well as spiritual. They also believe that politics has a role to play in the creation of a just society, and that politics and faith are not rigidly separable. At the same time, however, they share some of the traditional women's more spiritualized understanding. Moreover, they are more ambiguous about the connections between capitalism, structural sin, socialism, and the kingdom of God than women in the CEB vanguard.

CONCLUSIONS

Much evidence suggests that the reception of the liberationist message has been mixed. In addition to the variety of interpretations cited here and in Burdick's study, we could cite Hewitt's finding that only 39 percent of São Paulo CEB members even adopted liberationist language (e.g., chose to identify Christ as "liberator" rather than Savior or Son of God) in 1984 (Hewitt 1991, 92).[25] Other studies have reached similar conclusions about the limited "conversion" to liberation theology in Colombia and Venezuela, Chile and Peru.[26]

As we saw earlier, some pastoral agents credit women with "saving" the project of the Popular Church and others decry them as subverting it. Women have certainly been instrumental in the creation of the CEBs, and by their high level of participation they have necessarily helped determine how successful consciousness-raising has been. If they deserve credit for building the CEBs, does it follow that due to their presence, consciousness-raising has "failed"?

That conclusion rests on the assumption that religion is gendered, and in a particular way—that women's religious personalities are likely to be conservative or traditional. In fact, the evidence above suggests that women in the CEBs cannot be categorized so easily. Rather, their religious personalities span a fairly wide spectrum, from the conventional stereotype of the traditional Catholic woman to the surprisingly politicized and sometimes fiery liberationist.

Religious *behavior* appears to be significantly gendered, then, but religious *personality* does not. While it is true that only a minority of the women are liberationists, this may be related less to gender than to religious personality. This conclusion gains credence from the observation that while some liberationist men have passed through the CEBs in Santo Antônio on their way to more explicit political or trade unionist work, those men who remain active as members of the council, liturgy groups, and so on, tend to be closer in their attitudes to the traditional women than to the liberationist ones.[27] In Iracema's CEB, the two most active men were so religiously conservative that she and several samaritan religionists were frequently at loggerheads with them over consciousness-raising, the content of lay-led liturgies, and social movement organization. Thus the very strongest argument for a gendered response—that women would tend to cluster in one or two personality types hostile to liberationist ideas—seems implausible.

Nonetheless, the examples above suggest that the three religious personalities and their responses are framed by a common value of other-orientedness that may be related to women's caregiving roles and to the cultural expectations of "womanhood" described in the previous chapter. While the specific content of their value emphases ranges from charity to neighborly love to social justice activism, all three can be seen as variations on the theme of caretaking and nurturing. It is only in this much looser sense that their religiosity can be considered "gendered." Yet this common element may also have important and somewhat surprising implications for the political, rather than strictly religious, impact of the CEBs. As noted in the previous chapter, different political values or patterns of behavior were also hidden in the common theme of a "mother's heart." The following chapter explores the ways in which the minority of liberationist women have exploited women's common other-oriented values and their shared cultural identity as women to mobilize this religiously and politically diverse group in ways that an appeal to class solidarity probably never could.

FIVE

Ties That Bind

Political Attitudes
and Social Mobilization in CEBs

Brazil's most recent period of military rule ended with the indirect election of a civilian president in 1985.[1] In the ten years leading up to that election, the country had witnessed the growing organization of civil society. Trade unions organized a series of strikes in 1978, 1979, and 1980, and ultimately created a new, independent peak trade union organization and a leftist workers' party, the PT. Social movements demanding containment of inflation, day care and health care, education, and sanitation took to the streets. *Favela* and neighborhood associations emerged in poor areas of many large cities. When indirect presidential elections were announced, a massive movement to demand direct elections (*Diretas já*) was the response. Prominent bishops and clergy supported the emergence of civil society, linking the Popular Church to this oppositional and at times leftist political activity.

When I arrived in the area in 1986, Santo Antônio had a reputation for being *quente*—a hotbed of the liberationist church and of leftist political activity. Dom Angêlico, the region's outspoken bishop and a close associate of São Paulo's well-known liberationist Archbishop Dom Paulo Evaristo Arns, mingled radical political analysis with Catholic symbolism in his pamphlets, homilies, and interviews with the press. His PT sympathies were not disguised. Padre Chico and many of the pastoral agents who worked with him in the CEBs devoted much of their time to and had close connections with the church's Workers' Pastoral (*Pastoral Operária*) and the Workers' Party (PT). In previous years, the region had also supported all the new expressions of civil society: collecting food for the strikers in 1980, organizing a caravan to Brasília to demand *Diretas Já,* and lobbying for housing, health care, child care, and many other issues.

With its radical leadership and political effervescence, Santo Antônio and Itaim Paulista seemed to be examples of liberationist success in empowering the poor as active agents of history working for social justice. They represented the hope with which the Popular Church began: that the CEBs could change religious attitudes and symbolism, and thereby build political consciousness. This, in turn, would facilitate poor people's self-organization into collective movements for social change and perhaps ultimately—with the emergence of the PT—into a cohesive, leftist voting bloc.

In fact, the CEBs never fully lived up to these lofty expectations, and it is doubtful whether they ever could have done so. Their electoral impact, especially, is limited by the small share of the electorate their members represent—about 1.8 percent in 1994 (Pierucci and Prandi 1995, 28). The CEBs have also proven unable to recruit massively for a single party, the PT (Bruneau and Hewitt 1989; Drogus 1992). Nonetheless, in 1994, CEB members were significantly more likely than a random sample of Brazilians to vote for leftist candidates, especially the PT (Pierucci and Prandi 1995, 32). Moreover, in areas such as Santo Antônio, they also successfully mobilized significant numbers of individuals into radical-appearing social movements.

Were the CEBs more successful at raising political consciousness than they were at disseminating liberationist religious ideas? What explains the success of the social movements, and particularly their success in recruiting individuals who did not all share implicit liberationist faith or political beliefs? The answer may lie not in the CEBs' ability to generate a uniform class consciousness, but rather in the lay leadership's ability to produce a discourse capable of unifying individuals despite quite dissimilar political ideas. In this case, the women's ability to discuss the movements in terms that touched their common cultural notions of womanhood and a related continuum of religious values (charity-love-social justice) unified them where liberation theology could not.

POLITICAL CONSCIOUSNESS

Liberation theology cannot be reduced to its politics. Not even the most politically committed theologian or pastoral agent would claim that changing political beliefs is the primary function of the CEBs. Moreover, most theological writing, and even much of the didactic material produced for use in the CEBs, is less clear about the content of "liberating" political beliefs than about "liberating" religious symbols. Daniel Levine argues that only one of several models of CEBs existing throughout Latin America, "the radical ideal," is highly politicized and emphasizes class conflict. Brazil's CEBs, in contrast, mostly follow the "sociocultural model" which is much less explicitly political, and certainly less confrontational (Levine 1992, 48).

Yet even this model of CEBs, as Levine argues, envisages fostering political change. At the least, the idea behind the sociocultural model of the CEBs is that the groups will foster a change of attitudes on a personal and, eventually, a cultural level, and that these new attitudes will be conducive to democratization, social justice, and political empowerment of the poor.[2] For example, by promoting democratization of religious authority, the groups model a more participatory, democratic political system. Similarly, by promoting community solidarity they can foster attitudes conducive to social justice.

Sociocultural CEBs thus seek to act "as seedbeds of a new, democratic culture and social order, providing norms that legitimate equality and the promotion of social justice . . ." (Levine 1986b, 14).

Teresa Caldeira claims more specifically that the CEBs in Brazil seek to create a political ethos that will challenge the tradition of electoral populism (Caldeira 1986–87, 44). Charles Reilly argues that the political project of the CEBs can be summarized as a kind of "societal populism," in contrast to the "state populism" typified by the regime of Getúlio Vargas, for example (Reilly 1986, 44–46). State populism involved manipulation of mass support and occasional mobilization of working class groups through state-controlled channels and on behalf of a political and economic project defined by the populist leader and the economic elite. Societal populism, in contrast, envisions working class mobilization in movements of their own creation for autonomous participation in the decision-making processes of society.

The concept of societal populism resonates well with liberation theology's emphases on social justice and the idea of the poor as agents of history.[3] In other words, the poor in the CEBs must be mobilized to participate politically, to make their demands heard in the government. As the theologians see it, the objective is not merely to mobilize individuals, but also to mobilize people *as a class*—to transform the "intuition" of class consciousness into a reality.

The specific aim of consciousness-raising is the cultivation of a systematized, articulate class consciousness from the components of popular consciousness. More diffusely, it seeks to enhance political interest, autonomy, and "empowerment" of the working class. Members should gain an increased interest in participating politically and an increased sense of efficacy. The elements of class consciousness and empowerment go together in the ideal or model. They can be separated for purposes of analysis, however, in order to develop a clearer, more complete evaluation of the relative success of political *conscientização*.

Religious Personality, Popular Consciousness, and Consciousness-Raising

Liberation theologians see their task as "recuperating" elements of popular religious and political consciousness, and transforming it into a more clearly class-based consciousness by "systematizing" people's intuitive understanding of society and its structures (L. Boff 1984a, 4; C. Boff 1984, 6–7). The task is not easy, because as we saw in the previous chapter, existing attitudes include some that are conducive to such efforts and others that inhibit them. As Frei Betto remarks:

> it is common for some members of the community to start to repeat certain terms . . . like "liberation," without however apprehending the content that terminology has in the mind of the (pastoral) agent. . . . In fact, the absorption of vocabulary and even the statement of social injustices translate into a new praxis or lead to discernment of existing conditions only with difficulty. . . . The agent wants to teach, convert, politicize, but he achieves nothing but modifying the common expressions of popular religion. (Betto 1981, 70, my translation)

While a communitarian, outward-looking faith helps liberationist religionists to embrace liberation theology, a more individual, inward-looking orientation leads traditional religionists to reject or simply reinterpret the new symbols, even if both groups use the same words.

Similarly, secular popular consciousness contains a mix of beliefs. Recognition of the existing class structure of society, a sense that the existing economic distribution is unfair, and a feeling of compassion often expressed through individual acts of charity could all contribute to consciousness-raising. Teresa Caldeira's study of working-class consciousness shows that these elements are indeed widespread in existing popular political culture (Caldeira 1984, 154–55, 196–97).[4] But there are a number of obstacles to the CEBs' project as well. These include a popular sense that rich and poor are natural and complementary social categories, a preference for individual rather than collective strategies of social ascension, and a belief that the poor cannot exercise power politically—or cannot do so safely (Caldeira 1984, 248, 151–52,154–55, 169, 197–98, 253–55).

These themes indicate the potential complexity of political consciousness-raising. All three religious personalities described in the previous chapter have at least some basis for a positive response: the charity-love-social justice value triad suggests a basis for each type to respond to calls for class solidarity. But some traditional and samaritan religionists rejected the idea of social sin because they also believe that the rich-poor divide is natural and even functional. They are, therefore, less likely than the liberationist women to respond to political consciousness-raising.[5]

CEBs' Impact on Beliefs about Politics

As with liberationist religious language, a near unanimity in the use of radical political phrases proved to cover an array of political ideas. Nearly everyone spoke of a "social pyramid" in which the few wealthy crush the many poor, the idea that the poor must unite, criticisms of "capitalism" and especially of "capitalists," and the idea that the poor must struggle to improve their lot. Used by traditional and many samaritan religionists, however, this language seems to reflect the kind of unreconstructed popular consciousness Caldeira describes rather than the conscientization to which the CEBs aspire.

Traditional women are the least likely to adopt "conscientized" political attitudes. In chapter 4, we saw that traditional women like Margarita describe the division of society into rich and poor as natural. As Eloisa says, "The poor man, *coitado* [poor thing], he'll never be rich. He'll never be equal to the rich man. . . . Wealth doesn't come to everybody" (interview, Oct. 1986). They may join the other women in arguing that Brazilian workers deserve better wages, but traditional women are quick to distinguish between "deserving" and "undeserving" workers.

Similarly, they reject the notion that capitalist relations of production are in and of themselves exploitative. Cristina, for example, contrasts her own view with that of many CEB members: "What happens a lot, I see this a lot, is the poor curse the rich man because he's rich. That's what happens a lot. And I don't agree with that. Because lots of times the rich man is rich, but not because he's bad. Sometimes he's rich because he really worked and achieved what he has by working" (Nov. 1986). Neide makes a similar argument in self-defense. As owners of rental property, she and her husband are "rich" relative to the rest of the community. She finds the CEB's criticisms of the rich a personal affront and responds that, like many better-off people, they worked hard for what they have (Sept. 1986).

Several traditional women argued that the existence of rich and poor is not only natural, but also necessary, because rich and poor serve complementary functions in society. Cristina said, "I think it's logical that in a society one has more than another, provided all have enough to get along." And she added: "My father always worked in industry. But he never [tried to be equal to the boss]. He said, I don't work to enrich the boss. I work to help the boss, and to help myself. It's an exchange. The boss needs you, and you need the boss" (Nov. 1986). Margarita also expressed her belief that "It's necessary to have *grandes* [rich people]," in part because cooperation between rich and poor enables the poor to make their way up in the world (Oct. 1986).[6]

Liberationist women were much more critical of existing economic relations as their position on structural sin might suggest. They were much more apt to use the term "injustice" when describing rich-poor relations and to argue that the poor were fighting for their "rights"—a concept that the traditional women rarely used.[7] Iracema cited the people's right to better living conditions and the injustice of inequitable land distribution. She argued that an agrarian reform was not only desirable, but the only proper action the government could take. The people thus should actively demand that such measures be taken (field notes, Oct. 1986). In contrast, traditional religionist Eloisa agreed that an agrarian reform would be desirable to alleviate the suffering of the poor, but saw this as a largely philanthropic action by the government, justified merely by necessity (Oct. 1986).

Only the traditional women described the status quo as natural or desirable; but at the same time, only a handful even of the liberationist women had the well-developed notion—toward which *conscientização* aspires—that rich and poor have opposing interests. Commenting on the elections, Adelita noted that "the rich can only be expected to protect their own interests, and we have to do the same" (field notes, May 1986).[8] Maria dos Anjos believes that justice for the rural poor will be achieved "only when the power of the *latifundistas* is broken" (Oct. 1986).[9] Catarina and Cíntia also express the conviction that there is a fundamental clash of interests between rich and poor (Sept. 1986). Other liberationist women were less certain that there is a structural or fundamental conflict.

Most samaritans did not discard the possibility that in a well-functioning society rich and poor would work together for the mutual benefit of all, coming much closer to the understanding of the traditional women. Rather, they were likely to say that this does not happen in practice because of the hard-heartedness of the wealthy, because they do not "take pity" on

the poor, as Maria Angela says (Nov. 1986). Young Marcela believes that cooperation between classes is possible because
there are some "good" rich people who are willing to help the
poor. She cites the case of a wealthy, popular radio personality
who tried to run for the presidency in 1989, but was disquali-
fied: "But isn't there after all someone like Sílvio Santos, a rich
guy—and how! A guy who's pretty egotistical, but he does
what he can for people. And the people just say bad things
about him" (Nov. 1986). When we recall that this group interpreted a liberationist transformation of society in terms of the
conversion of individual hearts, it is not surprising that they
also attribute the failure of rich-poor cooperation to the moral
failings of individuals.

Criticism of the distribution of economic benefits that attributes this situation to the good or evil of wealthy individuals
might be the early fruit of *conscientização*. Moral condemnation of the greedy, hard-hearted rich, however, is also a strong
part of the political consciousness of most Brazilian workers,
even if they have not been exposed to consciousness-raising
(Caldeira 1984, 154–55, 215). Traditional women, too, express
the opinion that the poor are, as a rule, more merciful and
charitable than the rich. Thus, most CEB members' consciousness seems "unreconstructed" on this point.

Women of all three types also express some shared desires for social change. The women uniformly state that workers should be better off, with more health care, day care, food,
and services provided to give all Brazilians a minimally decent
standard of living. Traditional and samaritan religionists express these aspirations rather vaguely, not seeming to conceive
of them as attainable political objectives. Many simply varied
Eloisa's theme that "If the rich would share with the poor, that
would be great, wouldn't it?"(Oct. 1986).[10]

The traditional and samaritan religionists were also most
likely to include more moral or spiritual goals for the society

in their visions of the future. Marcela described her utopia as a brotherhood of "black, white, Latin American, Japanese, all there just embracing each other to say, how great that you're here" (Nov. 1986). Eloisa said that something should be done to improve the lot of the poor and "alleviate their suffering." While she believes material equality is unattainable in this life, she does express a more spiritualized hope for equality: "We should all be equal like this, in terms of love, in our living, in peace, at peace with everyone. Even being weak [poor], but that is to say we should know how to love, to be humble, to have a good heart toward others. That's how I see it" (Oct. 1986).

Liberationist religionists also expressed aspirations for greater Christian fellowship, caring, and so forth, but they, along with one samaritan, also put their aspirations in much more concrete and more political terms. They were often unclear about what exactly "equality" would look like, as we saw with "socialism" in the previous chapter. Most liberationist women, like Maria dos Anjos, wavered between adamant statements that "everybody should be equal, and have everything equal," and the more moderate conviction that "the workers should be able to 'move up' three or four steps" (Oct. 1986). Given the extremes of wealth and poverty in Brazil, it is perhaps not surprising that their conviction that social conditions could be changed is limited to a desire to narrow, rather than eliminate, the gap.

Some women also differed from the rest in adding the category of equality of rights to their vision of society. Marli, a samaritan, described the ideal of a "new society," and said that a PT victory would be a step toward the realization of this utopia because "if the party, the PT, the Workers' Party, if it won it would reform the laws. It would find a way to make everybody equal. There wouldn't be rich or poor" (Nov. 1986).

But when pressed to explain further what she meant by the idea that "everybody" would be "equal," Marli rejected an economic definition. She said that of course there would always be rich and poor in economic terms, but that rich and poor would be equal "in passing through different places"; that is, they would be treated equally, and everyone would have an equal right to enter clubs, shops, offices, and demand service. Whatever their economic condition people would, as she said at another point, "be given value." They would have "a turn and a say" (Nov. 1986). Liberationist religionist Zélia similarly stressed the idea of equality before the law, adding that people in the CEBs were protesting in order to gain their rights (Oct. 1986).

Perhaps the most persuasive evidence of an attitudinal difference between the traditional and liberationist women appears in their strategies for attaining their personal future aspirations. All of the women aspire to individual upward mobility—a better house, car, or job—as well as hoping that the lot of the poor generally will improve. Only the liberationist and some samaritan religionists connect individual and class mobility to a *political* strategy, however. The rest pursue individual and familial strategies of social ascension, while expressing a vague hope that the rich will "look at" and help the poor.

Most poor *paulistanos* believe that health, hard work, saving, family cooperation, and education are the keys to a strategy of individual or familial social ascension (Caldeira 1984, 169). Nearly all of the traditional and samaritan religionists, as well as one liberationist religionist, mentioned at least one of these factors as essential to improving their economic fortunes.[11] In contrast, they failed to mention collective strategies while translating the CEB's themes of class struggle into personal and familial terms.

Traditional women utilize vocabulary current in the CEBs in their accounts of how one can "improve" in life. Margarita, for example, says, "What makes us remain poor is our *acomodismo*" (Oct. 1986). In the CEB, *acomodismo* [adj., *acomodado*] is often used in a sense similar to "cooptation," to refer to people who are unwilling to join in the collective struggle of the working class. Margarita soon made it clear that she had a rather different picture of a person who is *acomodado* in mind. For her and other traditional women, a person who is *acomodado* refuses to work hard pursuing an individual strategy of social ascension. Margarita cites her own case as a counter-example: she worked at every available kind of employment to enable her children to achieve a higher level of training. Cleide notes the familial strategy of hard-working Japanese immigrants, and contrasts them ["You never see them poor, or begging"] with "lazy" Brazilians (Aug. 1986).

What is perhaps most striking and suggestive in terms of specifically political attitudes is the willingness of the traditional women to extend an individualist approach even into arenas, like salary negotiation, where others might see the benefits of collective organization. Margarita, Clara, Neide, and Cristina all rejected collective action by workers (particularly strikes) as an effective strategy for improving the economic position of the poor.[12] This rejection may stem in part from the realistic conviction that most collective action by workers has limited possibilities for success. It also involves a moral condemnation of collective action as too conflictual:

> You have a right to demand your rights, to have a fair salary in line with what you do. . . . That much you have. But it's not for the employee to struggle, fight with the boss, in order to earn as much as the boss. . . . That's why I think there shouldn't be so much rivalry. Nobody stops to talk. That's why I'm usually against strikes. Because what I see is

that there's hardly been a meeting, you know? You just try one or two times, and you're on strike. (Nov. 1986)

In place of this conflictual model, traditional women suggest the rapprochement of individual workers and employers. When they perceive the possibility of collective action at all, it is in terms of a nonconflictual, classically corporatist model of harmonious worker-employer relations. Margarita explains that it is not necessary to "overcome" capitalism. As a worker talks with the employer, the employer will understand the conditions of the worker's life and the need for better pay.

> Through your dialogue with him, it won't be necessary to change capitalism. Because helping the worker, through a dialogue, and a good salary, and teaching him . . . he'll learn how to work with that salary he's earning. After a while, he won't be just a worker who wants to earn money to eat and drink. Because he's a worker who's been given the mentality to work to build. To build! And he passes that on to others. So capitalism affirms itself, and it's like a big family. It's not like employees, it's like a family. In the firm, it's the construction of a family. (Oct. 1986)

Traditional women, then, espouse a strategy of social ascension that involves both individual initiative and—at most—nonconflictive collective bargaining between workers and employers. Their emphasis is on individual motivation and merit.

Only the liberationist religionists came close to viewing social ascension for the individual as inseparable from the advancement of the class as a whole. Liberationist religionists and their families do not eschew strategies to improve their own individual well-being, but only they considered such strategies ineffective and meaningless apart from the struggle for better conditions for all workers. The class nature of social ascension is mildly expressed, and it may be stretching the point to argue

that their claims to be "struggling on behalf of all the workers" really represent a significant move toward the radical
model of class consciousness.[13] Even so, liberationist religionists alone were more likely even to make this assertion.

Some of the liberationist religionists expressed the idea
of commitment to collective rather than only familial social ascension with particular clarity. Iraci, for example, recalled her
experience as a factory worker: "I worked at Philco, I was a
metal worker. But at that time, I didn't have the least bit of
consciousness. I contributed a lot because I always fought, but
I always fought alone. . . . To get me to shut up, they offered
me a raise. And I found that so unfair because I would have
to hide it from my coworkers. I didn't accept it, but I didn't
motivate anyone else to fight for the same raise. I just rejected it . . . I didn't see that all of the workers have to struggle
together" (Nov. 1986). Maria dos Anjos said that she could
pursue an individual strategy of upward mobility, but added
that only "one or two" could make it in that way, while her
objective is "improvement for the whole working class"
(Oct. 1986). Similarly, Catarina recalled that when she began to
participate in the CEB, her reflection focused on her own individual and family problems. Now she says she has developed
a more "communitarian" view. "Now I want to achieve progress for the whole class, for all of the workers," she says, "not
just for my own family" (Sept. 1986).[14]

This theme is only one of several that reveal the limits
of political consciousness-raising in the CEBs. As with the religious themes in the previous chapter, the political ideas ex-
plored here seem to meet resistance not because the women
as women reject them, but because different personal and religious attitudes—different combinations of elements common to popular consciousness—predispose some individuals
to accept the new ideas and inhibit others from doing so.
In fact, the pattern seems to duplicate the one described in

chapter 4, with only liberationist women embracing the CEBs' ideas of consciousness, while other women expressed opinions that were not noticeably different from the general popular consciousness or, in the case of traditional women, were even quite politically conservative. If the CEBs' effectiveness in generating a particular type of consciousness has been slight, they have been significantly more effective in the broader goal of enhancing members' political interest and sense of empowerment.

Political Interest and Empowerment

Chapters 1 and 2 noted some cultural and social science stereotypes of women—especially poor, religious housewives—as politically disinterested and marginal. The CEBs successfully legitimized politics as an area of discussion and knowledge for women. This in itself is an important achievement, since the interviewees affirmed nearly unanimously that prior to their involvement in the CEB, they had no interest in politics.[15]

The active women frequently comment on the lack of political knowledge and interest among newer recruits to the CEBs. They generally follow up such remarks by adding, "But of course we ourselves were that way when we started." Maria dos Anjos referred to her family background to explain why she had not participated in any political activities before joining the CEB:

> My father was a real political person, but he was one of those *macho* guys. He was a man who only had daughters. Only he participated, because he was a man, and so women had no right to participate in any struggle. . . . But when I came here, the struggles were beginning in the church, and that sparked the fire. [In Paraná] I hadn't participated much because I didn't have a chance. My father held us back a lot, you know? (Oct. 1986).

Although this history clearly contrasts with that of Zélia who felt her immigrant parents encouraged her to learn about politics, both women said that they had not actually begun to participate in political activities until they became involved through the CEB.

Voting is obligatory, so every Brazilian with an elector's title must at least cast a ballot. Although they fulfilled their civic requirements, most women said they had little interest in the process. Most echoed in some way Chica's remarks: "When I didn't participate in the community, I didn't care much about voting. I voted because I was obligated, but I didn't pay attention. [Laughter] I'll go vote, because I'm of age, you have to vote, but I wasn't even interested. Now I vote with much more consciousness . . . " (Dec. 1986). Catarina said she had never participated before and, although curious about political problems, she had never made an effort to become involved (Sept. 1986). Maria dos Anjos said she always just voted the way her husband told her to (field notes, Oct. 1986).[16] Only Marli claimed that she had always had some interest in politics, and that was not very serious: "I used to talk about politics a lot, but I hardly understood anything, you know? Talking just to talk, sure, but without understanding. [Laughter] My husband and I, we two used to talk about it, but I didn't understand, and neither did he" (Nov. 1986). Although she always liked to "shoot the breeze" about politics, Marli, like the rest of the women, said that her participation had only become more profound in the CEB.

While most of the women claim subjectively that they now possess a greater knowledge of and interest in political issues, the CEBs have had only limited success in encouraging members to participate in general political information meetings, campaign rallies, and so on.[17] W. E. Hewitt found, for example, that only 23 percent of CEB members regularly participated in consciousness-raising groups (Hewitt 1991, 48). Similarly, aggregate data suggests that progressive dioceses like São Paulo have not been successful in encouraging practicing Catholics to become politically involved: they were actually less likely than their nonpracticing peers to participate in political rallies (Bruneau and Hewitt 1989, 50).

In Itaim Paulista, the CEBs sponsored numerous candidate meetings and political debates prior to the congressional and gubernatorial elections in November 1986. Most meetings attracted only a handful of members.[18] Yet it is remarkable that, contrary to expectations based on the political profile of working-class Brazilian women, most of those in attendance were usually women. At one debate between two candidates for the legislature, for example, twenty-two of thirty-two people attending were women (field notes, Aug. 1986). About half of those were women who regularly attend the *Clube de Mães*. Most were liberationist or samaritan religionists; few traditional religionists translate their subjective assessments of greater political interest into active participation in specifically political meetings. Nonetheless, the low level of overall participation must be seen in context. Many liberationists and more activist samaritans have found a niche for greater political participation in the CEBs. Although the CEBs have not motivated *all* of their members to pursue greater political awareness, they have opened important spaces and offered encouragement to those who wish to do so. This is especially important to women who often feel that a lack of opportunities hinders their political involvement.

In addition to legitimizing political interest, the CEBs also have contributed to a sense of political empowerment. Grassroots organizations like CEBs can play a crucial role in giving groups with little political opportunity or experience— the poor, the less educated, women—a chance to develop self-confidence in a public arena.[19] They can help to foster specific skills, such as public speaking, organizational skills, and the ability to negotiate the public bureaucracy, as well. The CEBs in Itaim Paulista fulfilled all of these functions.

The CEBs' importance in providing these opportunities for poor *women* cannot be overemphasized. As religious organizations, the CEBs possess a legitimacy in the eyes of both the women and their husbands that no movement or party could claim. This is crucial to facilitating women's mobilization. The presence of religious personnel made unfamiliar political activities easier for many. For women whose husbands object to politics as unseemly for their wives, the CEB provides a religious cover. Many respondents said, "He can't stop me from going to church!" Familial conflicts tend to escalate as the perceived "religious" component of activity decreases in proportion to the "political" element.

Carmen Macedo stresses the way CEB members value the groups' educative function, and we have already seen that many take advantage of literacy and other classes (Macedo 1986, 237). Scott Mainwaring points out their role in developing popular leadership (Mainwaring 1989, 157). And chapter 3 gave the example of Adelita, who credited the CEB with literally broadening her horizons by teaching her how to move about the city beyond her neighborhood.

In addition to concrete skills and experience, the CEBs have been important in fostering the women's *belief* in the efficacy of a united effort. Every one of the interviewees believed that the poor could have some power to change society—a finding that contrasts with Caldeira's description of a dominant political ethos in which the poor perceive themselves as weak and at the mercy of a strong government (Caldeira 1984, 247). At the very least, the CEBs have given all of their members a sense that they can have some collective control over their destinies.

The strength of this belief does vary across the different religious types. The liberationist women are most confident, although even they believe that the people will be truly strong only once apathy and lack of consciousness can be overcome. Some of the traditional and samaritan religionists expressed the conviction that in the face of government opposition, the people might not be sufficiently strong to attain their objectives: "I think the people have a lot of strength, if they fight. But also if the government doesn't want to do it, well, then there's the strength of the people up to a point, and the strength of the powerful, as they say. So it would be a big battle for the people. They have a lot of strength, but so do the white-collar people . . . "(Aug. 1986).

Moreover, differences appear in the women's interpretation of "unity" as the source of the people's strength. For the liberationist women, unity clearly has a class-based dimension. They refer to the unity of "the workers," of "the oppressed," or of "the poor" (interviews, Sept. 1986; field notes, Oct., Dec. 1986). In contrast, some of the traditional women, like Margarita and Cristina, define a united people in fairly class-neutral terms, as an aggregation of rich and poor working for a common cause. Caldeira found this to be a common attitude among her respondents. Margarita especially seemed to de-politicize even the concept of "unity," applying it to friendship, mutual aid, and supportiveness.[20]

This difference is not surprising given what we already know of the respondents' attitudes toward some forms of collective action, like trade unions. Yet even the women who seem farthest from class consciousness perceive some acceptable means by which poor people can effectively help one another by working together. Margarita said that people could boycott distributors who were refusing to accept government food coupons for milk (field notes, Sept. 1986). And she cited organizing movements and passing petitions as ways in which people could organize themselves to bring about change (Oct. 1986). Several women stressed that after electing officials, the people must continue to hold them responsible, petition them, and make demands for what they want (July, Nov. 1986).

It is not clear how much this sense of empowerment directly results from the process of consciousness-raising per se. In fact, given the very concrete terms in which women like Margarita described their belief that the "united people" could bring about change, it may be fair to say that empowerment has accompanied the concrete victories of particular mutual aid projects and social movements. This seems especially likely when we recall that the traditional women did not seem to view larger areas of social change as subject to the people's collective action. They did have a sense of increased ability to effect change locally—precisely the kind of change the social movements bring about. The following sections explore the ways in which a sense of empowerment has played out in electoral politics and in social movements.

WOMEN AND THE PT VOTE

Brazil's military government was in many respects unique. Perhaps one its most unusual features was the preservation—albeit in a manipulated form—of electoral politics. The military outlawed parties exising before 1964 and replaced them with two parties of its own creation: ARENA (Aliança de Renovação Nacional), which was to be the party of the government, and the MDB (Movimento Democrático Brasileiro), intended to serve as a controlled voice for the opposition. These two parties were allowed to dispute legislative seats, although the military controlled the presidency, while governors and the mayors of state capitals were elected indirectly by the state legislature. The military also revised electoral rules whenever necessary to circumscribe MDB victories because even in this highly manipulated context, Brazilians took advantage of elections to express their dissatisfaction with military rule by voting for the MDB.

Military rule simplified the electoral decision for individuals and grassroots groups: vote either for the government or for the opposition. With the return to multiparty elections, the CEBs and other groups in civil society faced a number of difficult decisions about their potential relationship with the emerging parties (Mainwaring 1989, 174). Multiparty politics raised a plethora of complex choices that grassroots leaders were in many cases unprepared to deal with, yet escaping the party question was nearly impossible. As one of the few autonomous organized groups in civil society, the CEBs were besieged by parties seeking to make them into an electoral base.

Debates arose over the degree to which the CEBs should address electoral issues at all, over the extent to which a specific party could be endorsed while maintaining the CEBs intact, and over the propriety of conflictual partisan politics as an activity for members of a universal church whose critique of society was more moral than politically strategic. Liberationists are divided over the issue of the relationship between the CEBs and political parties. Many priests are skeptical of political parties and fear that they will manipulate the CEBs (Galletta, 143; Pierucci, 369–70; Mainwaring 1986, 202). A few take an anarchist position; most believe that popular social movements are more valuable than political parties (Pierucci, 532; Mainwaring 1989, 174).

The debate has raged since the late 1970s. At the 1989 National Encounter, opinion ranged from the view that the CEBs were no longer playing a political role, to Clodóvis Boff's call for a "party-political pastoral" enabling Christians to "create a party that is popular, transforming and democratic."[21] The practice in individual CEBs is thus bound to vary widely. In some, the desire to avoid partisanship and favor a more ethical approach to politics led groups to limit their involvement in politics (Galletta 1985, 161, 165).

The CEBs in Santo Antônio, like some others, identified with the *Partido dos Trabalhadores* (PT). One reason for the strong CEB-PT link in many cases is the perception that the Popular Church and the party share a commitment to working from the base of society upwards—a commitment that most other Brazilian parties do not share. Indeed, Frei Betto claims that one principle of political consciousness strongly rooted in the CEBs is that "only that which is born from the base" is trustworthy, and in the context of Brazilian party politics, that means only the PT (Pierucci 1984, 14–15). The PT is perceived as having a "new practice," important aspects of which include direct democracy, anti-authoritarianism, little manipulation of electors, great responsibility given to the base, high value placed on popular culture, anti-dogmatism, and pluralism (Galletta 1985, 63).

Scott Mainwaring describes the "particular affinity" between the PT and the CEBs as follows:

> Indeed, it is difficult to even imagine the existence of the PT had grass-roots church groups not existed. The PT was inspired by progressive Catholic ideas emphasizing popular participation, grass-roots democracy, popular organization, and basic needs. Like the Popular Church, the PT placed greater emphasis on popular concerns than on liberal concerns such as electoral arrangements. In many parts of the country, grass-roots Catholic leaders played the predominant role in the PT. (Mainwaring 1989, 174)[22]

Of course, the coincidence in philosophy and structure is far from total. The PT includes many tendencies, of which the church faction (the so-called 113 group) is only one.[23] Others include Trotskyites and other Marxist groups who are often at odds with the 113 faction. The PT has also taken many bourgeois leftists into its fold, including environmentalists, feminists, and gay activists. In 1986, many church supporters of the PT were unaware that "their" party favored legalizing divorce and abortion. Others considered this less important than the party's credentials as an organization of the base committed to meeting basic needs.

The philosophical and structural similarities between the CEBs and the PT, and the perception that the church leadership in São Paulo and especially areas like Itaim support the PT, mean that adherence to the party has become a commonly used measure of CEB effectiveness and influence.[24] While the divisions and dilemmas in party and church make this debatable when one considers Brazilian CEBs in general, Santo Antônio's particular history makes it reasonable to assess the possible contribution of the CEBs to the formation of PT support (see chapter 2).

Support among activists there is quite high: eighteen of thirty women expressed support for the PT. All of the liberationist religionists supported the PT. All of the samaritans named the PT as their preferred party, although Marcela intended to split her vote between the PT and the PMBD, the historic opposition (Nov. 1986). One traditional religionist also supported the party. In contrast, only one traditional religionist, Neide, totally rejected the PT as a socialist party and its leader, Luís Ignácio da Silva (Lula), as a "crass" and "uneducated" man (Sept. 1986). Repeating the established pattern many traditional religionists expressed at least some favorable opinions about the PT, often using stock CEB language. The clear differences between the party's *ideas* and their own should alert us to the possibility that this support is merely superficial.

The communities exert a strong peer-group pressure for women to support the PT. In group meetings there is often virtually no overt dissent over the party issue. Traditional women, especially, may feel compelled to voice the same "line" as the others at meetings. The importance of peer pressure should be recognized especially when dealing with collective statements and interviews. Neide, for example, told me that she didn't support any particular party, but that she might vote for right-wing candidate Paulo Maluf. She mistrusts the PT leadership and criticizes Brazilians for wanting a socialist or communist government, which she sees as an expression of laziness. Shortly after privately explaining in detail her objections to the PT and socialism, however, she joined in a group discussion of the upcoming election by making a very typical pro-PT speech, although she did not refer to the party by name (interview and field notes, Sept. 1986). There is strong social pressure on women for consensus, and this is often reinforced by self-doubt about their opinions on public matters, especially if their level of literacy is low. In fact, it was often difficult to persuade women to offer their opinions privately. Even active participants often demurred when I asked to interview them, trying to direct me instead to the established leaders like Iracema and Zélia who would "know more about" things.

Traditional religionists all claimed to make their voting decisions based on the individual candidate rather than the party.[25] And they expressed admiration either for Lula or for other PT candidates who were perceived as working on behalf of the people (Nov. 1986). How little these choices had to do with shared ideology is clear from the fact that these individuals also expressed support for many candidates who were derided by their CEB colleagues as the candidates of "the bosses," such as center-right candidate Antônio Ermírio de Moraes, one of Brazil's wealthiest businessmen (Aug. 1986).

The apparent pro-PT consensus holds up in private only for the liberationists, some samaritans, and one traditional woman. Their support is most likely a result of the CEB's influence rather than any other social or economic factor. The respondents were considerably more likely than the local population in general to support the PT; for example, 60 percent compared to the 25.7 percent of residents in Itaim Paulista voted for the PT in 1986 (Lamounier 1986, 112). They were also at least three times as likely to support the PT as employed women or housewives in São Paulo, a figure that also applies when they are compared with *paulistanas* of low educational background (Avelar 1985, 149, 154). In fact, the support level for the PT is a bit higher than the 50 percent Hewitt found in lower-class CEB leaders in São Paulo (Hewitt 1985, 134). While the respondents do not all fit the category of CEB leaders, they *are* the most active participants and should therefore be the most susceptible to CEB norms, as they apparently are (Wald et al. 1988, 536).

But does the CEBs' ability to promote a leftist partisan identification imply a real move away from populist attitudes which are supposed to be especially pronounced among women? We have already seen that in many respects the respondents' political opinions have not changed. And while certain specific, apparently new attitudes have been inculcated along with support for the PT, it is not clear that some rather fundamental attitudes associated with populism have changed for most of the women who are professed PT supporters.

Expressed support for the PT is not equivalent to support for a well-defined political agenda: most women had only the vaguest idea of what the PT platform entailed. When asked why they supported the PT and what they expected it to do if elected, most of the women responded, at least in part, that it would "help poor people." The most active partisans, all liberationist religionists, had a clearer idea of the party's economic proposals, although even they were not aware of many aspects of the party platform. Most did not realize that "their" party supports legalized abortion and civil divorce, for example (Sept., Dec. 1986).

Much of the PT's legitimacy seems to stem from the perception that it is the party of the church. The church and the PT are strongly identified in the minds of many of the women, to the extent that several respondents commented that they support the PT because it is "on the side of the church" (Oct., Nov. 1986). Zélia is a liberationist religionist and one of the most active PT supporters. She says she believes in social-ism. But prominent on her list of reasons for partisanship is the fact that the church "supports" the PT (Oct. 1986). Samaritan Maria Angela explains her PT preference: "Isn't the church on the side of the poor? We have to choose a politics that works in favor of the church, and in favor of the poor" (Nov. 1986). Traditional religionist Eloisa's is the starkest case of professed partisanism based less on information and opinion than on the perception that the CEB supports the party. She did not know the PT was considered a leftist party, but said she felt sure it really wasn't—if it were, she added, Iracema would have said so at a meeting (Oct. 1986).

Given the tenuousness of many women's support for the PT and its divergence from their basic political attitudes, one must question the depth and durability of their support. The liberationist women who have accepted in some form the idea that Brazil needs a socialist transformation will probably con-tinue to support the PT long after the local church stops doing so. Indeed, they actively supported the candidacy of Luiza Erundina (PT) for mayor of São Paulo in 1989, despite the fact that the hierarchy would not support her (Sept. 1989). It is questionable whether the party allegiance of many of the other women would survive a withdrawal of church support for the PT. Without local pastoral agents stressing the importance of a pro-PT vote, it might be sustained mainly by habit and inertia for some; but the lack of group pressure might also dissolve the tenuous—and often only public—support of others.

As a largely nonideological vote for a group perceived as potentially helping the poor, the CEB pro-PT vote is in some ways similar to a traditional populist vote. At the same time, many of the liberationists and samaritans have also added new reasons to their lists of bases for choosing candidates, and these may represent something new in their overall approach to politics. For example, all of the women who support the PT stressed that the class origin of its candidates was important to them.[26] In a country where workers often look down on other workers as "poor and ignorant like us," the cultivation of the belief that workers can do something for themselves may be a new departure. This remains ambiguous, however, since it may also merely reflect the widespread belief noted above that the poor have better hearts than the rich.

Many also stressed the importance of having seen candidates participate in popular movements as evidence that they shared the struggle of the workers. In fact, this is often mentioned with respect to the choice of specific candidates for lower level posts (Sept. 1989). While populist candidates have always campaigned on their *obras,* the "works" they have performed for the population, the stress on candidates working *with* rather than *for* the people is new. Although it is unclear what the significance of this may be, it is possible that the populist model of the candidate dispensing largesse is being modified. For many women in the CEBs, candidates may now be evaluated more in terms of their willingness to listen to and work with autonomous citizens' groups.

It is thus difficult to assess what kinds of fundamental changes might be associated with support for the PT. Many respondents are still clearly looking for a candidate who will help poor people in some vaguely defined way. It is possible that if the local religious context shifts its support away from the PT and toward a more conservative party or candidate, many of these individuals will do so as well. Whether they do so or not may depend upon the candidate's ability to convince them that he or she has truly worked with or for the people in the past.

Given the nonideological nature of the women's party support and their rather low level of information about the party, it is not surprising that very few have become more active in party affairs. Only four are actually members of the party and only a slightly larger group participates in activities such as distributing campaign material and working the polls. That group is composed largely of liberationist women: Iracema, Zélia, Catarina, Cíntia, Maria dos Anjos, Joselina, Iraci, and Marli, a samaritan. Chica, also a samaritan, is occasionally recruited by Iracema and Marli for such activities.

The small size of this group could be linked to religious orientation since it is composed almost exclusively of liberationist religionists. However, gender is also almost certainly a factor inhibiting partisan activism for most women. Avelar concludes on the basis of a national survey that Brazilian housewives' domestic responsibilities and socialization are responsible for the fact that they are the group with the lowest level of participation in electoral campaigns (Avelar 1985, 116). Fanny Tabak and Moema Toscano found in a survey of *carioca* women voters that nearly 60 percent believed entry into a political party was not appropriate for women. A similar proportion disapproved of women's participation in electoral campaigns (Tabak and Toscano 1982, 38–39).

Women in Santo Antônio differ from Tabak and Toscano's sample because they unanimously affirmed that such political activities are appropriate for women "if they like them." However, while the respondents also said they thought politics important, many simply do not "like" it. This is true of both traditional and samaritan religionists. Cleide, for example, said that much of politics is *politicagem,* or dirty politics, a view that is widespread and—with regard to corruption and patronage—not unfounded (Aug. 1986). Chica also limits her electoral activities:

> I go to vote and all, you know? We have meetings with the women and I talk, no? But I don't really like politics. . . . And I have to say, it makes me nervous. I don't know how to talk about politics, because I don't like it. . . . People come and talk about those things, and I get nervous. And people disagree. I get mad, and I don't like that. I go to

some meetings because it's necessary, but I don't like it!
(Dec. 1986)

A distaste for the conflictual aspects of politics and an approach
to issues that springs from an ethic of love and help may combine to allow samaritans to view the PT as an appropriate political vehicle, but to limit their "politicization" and partisan
activism.

For some of the samaritan and traditional religionists, the
example of the more politicized liberationist women only reinforces their aversion to political activism. A general feeling that
politics are too dirty, immoral, and conflictual to be attractive
may be related to both gender socialization and, for some
women, their religious orientation. Although they would not
necessarily express it in this way, many seem to consider politics
still to be a "man's realm." Its ethos conflicts with the more
domestically-oriented women's image of appropriate female
behavior. As we shall see in chapter 6, the price of activism for
many of the liberationist activists has been dear, and their
problems reinforce the perception of politics as conflictual and
unfeminine.

Liberationist women's religious values and commitment
to the CEBs may help them to overcome the women's more
generalized distaste for politics in order to support a political party that they perceive as working along the lines of social
justice defined by the liberationist church. Women who do
not share the social justice commitment may remain more
susceptible to cultural influences and expectations that women
should avoid conflictual and dirty politics. At least, they have
no strong motivating force to overcome their habitual dislike
of party politics.

So the CEBs' impact on voting behavior overall seems to
be mixed. In Santo Antônio, they seem to have been remarkably but not uniformly able to orient people toward voting
for the PT—a conclusion reinforced by Pierucci and Prandi's

more recent finding that CEB members throughout Brazil are significantly more likely to support the PT. But the groups have probably been less successful in communicating and validating the PT's ideology, and support among many women is superficial and perhaps ephemeral. Moreover, very few women have been spurred on to overcome their own distaste and take advantage of the political opportunities the groups make available. The CEBs have been remarkably more successful, however, in encouraging even women who dislike politics to participate in social movements.

SOCIAL MOVEMENTS: WORKING CLASS OR MOTHERS' MOVEMENTS?

Before the transition back to civilian government created increased scope for electoral activity, the church promoted political participation through a wide variety of social movements. In Santo Antônio, these included day care, sanitation, water, street paving, street lights, housing, and squatter movements. Several of the movements, especially the squatter and day care movements, continued to be active nearly a decade after their initiation.

In contrast to the pattern of mixed response to consciousness-raising and party recruitment, the response to the social movements as new channels for political behavior was remarkably uniform and positive. This conclusion may seem surprising since the social movements were widely perceived as quite a radical form of political activity, yet few of the respondents who participated in the movements evince a particularly "radicalized" or "conscientized," class-based political consciousness. Moreover, such public, confrontational, and sometimes dangerous behavior seems out of keeping with accepted gender stereotypes, and we have already noted most women's dislike of and reluctance to participate in political activities that might result in conflict. Tabak and Toscano found that women in Rio reject participation in protests and demonstrations even more strongly than electoral activity (Tabak and Toscano 1982, 38–39). Some of the women in Santo Antônio who voiced qualms about conflictual electoral politics, however, recounted with great relish stories of demonstrations in which they stormed into a public official's office or faced armed police or fire hoses.

The social movements actually encompassed a broad range of women. Nearly all of the women have participated in at least some movements in some way. Many have participated in several of them. Although differences in the degree and form of the women's participation seem to correlate with their religious orientation and gender attitudes, women with very different religious, gender, and political positions found common cause in the social movements.

Given many women's failure to assimilate and internalize liberation theology's class analysis or political ideology, that ideology would seem a fragile basis for generating social movements. The way women describe their activism suggests that there was another reason for the high degree of acceptance of social movements: although outside observers sometimes saw the social movements as expressions of class consciousness or solidarity, the women themselves often interpreted the same movements as women's or, more specifically, mothers' movements. While acknowledging that their working-class status creates special problems for them as mothers, it was more often to this gender role rather than to class status alone that women referred in order to explain their unusual behavior.

All of the women share a common feminine language that reflects their concerns with children, family, and community, and their desire to help others. They also share a variety of feminine duties, as described in chapter 2, that give them a particular awareness of and perspective on neighborhood problems. Finally, despite the differences among the women's religious personalities, the family/traditional-love-social justice triad of values suggests a common theme of service and caregiving that is compatible with gender stereotypes, even though the specific interpretation of what such service might entail varies from one religious type to the next.

At some point in the interviews, nearly every woman directly expressed the sentiment that the social movements were a way of working on behalf of children—their own and all poor children more generally. We have already seen Simone's eloquent description of the vision her "mother's heart" makes her pursue in working for the children and the people more generally. Similarly, Iracema claimed, "It's not just for our own children. We are doing this for *all* our children. For all the children of Brazil" (Oct. 1986). Describing her leadership role in a movement to create a state-sponsored afterschool care program in the neighborhood an elderly woman said, "I don't have grandchildren, or children, or anything. But this is a necessary thing. We see that, and we're fighting for it, we want it. It doesn't matter if we have to spill blood. I want to see the struggle succeed" (July 1986). These three examples of the rationale behind the social movements come from liberationist religionists. But samaritan and traditional women offered the same rationale for their participation.

Samaritans often expressed their concern for abandoned children. Many noted a desire to work with these children and help them personally—an example of the face-to-face love that is a typical value of this group. Their movements for day care centers and an after-school care program were manifestations of this compassion. Both Simone and Fátima, a samaritan, described their efforts to form a sewing cooperative in the same terms. They did not need the work or income, but hoped the cooperative would help women and young girls from a nearby *favela* to learn a marketable skill (Dec. 1986).

Traditional women cited similar care-giving motivations. Neide described participating in the sanitation movement. She was moved primarily by the health hazards that the open garbage dumps posed "to poor people, and to children" (Sept. 1986). Cristina explains her participation in the movement as follows: "I like a movement that brings something good to the people. It was with Darcy, Father Darcy that got married, that we started that movement, and we even got rid of the garbage. I mean, that was a productive thing, it was good. The children that lived there, it was a shame to see" (Nov. 1986). Margarita's activities as a representative to the health center are motivated primarily by her concern for infants and children, and reflect her value emphasis on charity: her greatest efforts centered on trying to guarantee distribution of free milk for infants (Oct. 1986).

Despite the radical character imputed to the social movements by many observers at the time they took place, an examination of the motivations of the women in the CEBs who led and took part in these movements puts them in a rather different light. Liberationist women, who have been more responsive to political conscientization, do see a connection between the social movements and other forms of class-based politics, including voting for leftist political parties.[27] They may gently criticize their "less conscious" peers who perceive the objectives of particular movements in much narrower terms (field notes, July 1986).

As Catarina explained, most women in the CEBs do not perceive class-based sources of their problems or political solutions. She understood that few women share her more radical political consciousness. Nonetheless, she noted, women generally are eager to improve their neighborhood and to confront the problems that they and their families experience daily in a concrete way. Implicitly, she recognized other women's gender-based and religious bent toward caring for others

one-to-one or via charity. She concluded by noting that as a result, regardless of their political convictions, many women are
disponíveis—available for or open to—the social movements
(Sept. 1986). As a female leader of such movements, she could
understand other women's psychology and was willing to recruit them on that basis, even though she recognized that few
shared her own political convictions.

A shared construction of the movements based on gender
means that, for their part, even women who reject the political implications of liberation theology and the political options
of activists in the CEBs felt comfortable joining these public,
political activities. The less-conscientized women recognized
the movements as a way to care for children and community
in a larger arena. Traditional women perceived participation in
the movements as an extension of their habitual charitable activities in a new direction as well. They recognized that they
were acting politically, but in effect, political implications were
for them merely incidental. Theirs was much more a moral
than a political position.

The moral validity of the movements was reinforced by
church sponsorship. Had the movements not been linked to
the CEBs, it is unclear that as many traditional or samaritan
women could have been recruited. In Cristina's recollection,
for example, the sanitation movement is inextricably linked
with the presence of Father Darcy who encouraged the parish
to organize it. Neide said that she found it hard to get up the
courage to participate, but the fact that "the priests were together with us" in the movements made it easier (Sept. 1986).
In another community, a lay activist complained to me that
the women would "follow behind Sister Gabriela, crying, into
every movement." As a lay person and one who understood
the women's conflicts and difficulties, she could not make
them feel "guilty" enough to leave their domestic duties and
participate (July 1986).[28] Even the switch from a pastoral agent

to a lay person leading a movement reduced the incentive for women to participate, perhaps because it made the legitimacy of the movements as "charity" or "religious service" less clear.

None of the women, not even the traditional women, regarded the movements as nonpolitical. But the "helping" aspects of the movements, their construction as an extension of women's traditional religious and familial roles, and their locus in the church made it easier for women with no particular political or ideological consciousness to view the movements as a positive contribution to bettering the community— as, in essence, a moral or charitable act rather than a statement of political belief. Despite the very public character of their actions, the women could also then view their participation as compatible with their traditional gender roles while avoiding any conflict with their political principles.

While the shared gender-based discourse and religious legitimacy allowed women of different political opinions and religious types to unite, their differences continued to have some impact on the degree and form of their involvement. As we might have predicted, liberationist religionists emerge as the leaders of both the CEBs and the social movements. Iracema, Zélia, and women like them organize the movements and recruit others to join them. These women recount a history of moving from one issue to another as the goals of each movement are achieved. Most of the CEBs in Santo Antônio began with a sanitation movement, but once the garbage dumps were cleaned up, the women leading the Mothers' Clubs quickly found other neighborhood concerns around which to organize. In fact, many of these women began to form a regional women's association in 1986 in order to have a vehicle to continue a variety of social movements on an ongoing basis.

Samaritans present a more mixed profile of participation. A few, like Marli and Chica, work hand in hand with the liberationist religionists as organizers, though they are not generally the recognized leaders. For the most part, samaritans are the faithful rank and file of the movements. They "make up the number" when people are needed to protest at a government office, do the door-to-door canvassing, and so on. Like the first group, many move from issue to issue, participating in a wide range of movements.

A few samaritans have participated little in the movements. Most of these women have personal, specific reasons for their limited participation. Maria Angela is an example: she expresses support for all of the social movements her CEB has sponsored, but is only an occasional participant. Unlike most of the more active women, Maria Angela has two children in primary school. Given the limited school hours and variable schedules in Brazil, this severely restricts the time she can be away from home (Nov. 1986).

Traditional women, like samaritans, present a mixed profile. Many younger women with school-age children have not participated in social movements at all (June, Aug. 1986). But most traditional women have participated in at least one of the movements. A few, like Neide, have been active in nearly all (Sept. 1986).

Several characteristics distinguish the traditional women's participation. First, they are more selective in the movements in which they participate and are more critical of them. Cristina participated in a sanitation movement, but does not participate in the day-care movement. Her reasons for refusing reflect her traditional value emphasis:

> I don't agree much with the ideas of this day-care movement for just this reason: day care takes children out of the home. . . . In these four walls, with father and mother, he has their example. Not that he'll learn bad things at day care, no. But he won't have that idea of family. . . . Day

care, movements like that, I think the church is being too unilateral in these, you know? (Nov. 1986)

Similarly, Margarita participates in the land movement, but in keeping with her traditional values, she does not support the movement's use of illegal invasion as a tactic. Although she acknowledges the movement's oft-repeated claim that God gave the land to all in common, she believes that the "laws of man" which divided it up must be respected (May 1986). Traditional women will not automatically accept a movement that obviously goes contrary to their conservative political and moral beliefs, even when it is under church auspices and can be construed as charitable.

Traditional women may also confine their participation to certain activities. Only Neide mentioned participating in demonstrations. Margarita could not recall participating in any protests, but she attends meetings and provides follow-up and support work. She and Neide are both on the advisory board of the health post. They represent the CEB at meetings, make lists of needed equipment and medicine, and inform the Mothers' Club of the problems.

Other traditional women, whom I have not counted as movement participants, consider themselves part of the social movements because they view their charitable work as a form of participation. One older woman described her activities visiting the sick as part of the community's "health pastoral." Although the CEB has also promoted a movement to demand a health post as part of its pastoral activities, she has not participated in those activities. She sees her weekly visits, however, as part and parcel of the larger movement (Aug. 1986).

Religious orientation may combine with gender attitudes to explain these differences in participation. Women with a social justice orientation are far more likely to overcome gender stereotypes in order to become leaders and to be active in every movement. Among samaritan women, those with less traditional gender attitudes, like Marli, seem to be more active. Finally, traditional women are the most likely to limit themselves to charitable work, be selective in their support activities, and express reservations about the social movements. Their religious and political beliefs do not motivate them to lead, but the discourse of motherhood and linkage with the church gives them a basis for selective activism. But even most of the traditional women have found at least one movement they were willing to support actively.

CONCLUSIONS

The evidence from Santo Antônio suggests that those who believe that gender has had a conservatizing impact on the political objectives of the CEBs are only partially correct. As with religious symbolism, the tendency to adopt and act upon a liberationist political perspective seems to coincide with religious personality. The CEBs may generally produce significantly more PT support, and in Santo Antônio, such support was widespread although not universal among active women. The inability to "convert" traditional women to PT support and the tenuousness of many samaritans' support is probably an artifact of the same religious differences that made acceptance of liberation theology so uneven. Women's culturally defined identification with the private rather than the public spheres gives them an additional motivation for failing to support CEB-sponsored political activities, but liberationist religionists are generally able to overcome their reticence perhaps in part because their religious motivation and level of "consciousness" are so high. For them, and for some of the samaritans, the CEBs have provided a valuable outlet for political participation.

Although women's reluctance to become involved in politics is a part of the explanation for the CEBs' failure to generate more partisan political activism, gender seems to partly explain the success of the social movements, at least in the short term. The social movements' success in Itaim Paulista in the 1970s and early- to mid-1980s can be attributed in part to the women's ability to find a common acceptable definition of the movements that did not rely on a shared radical political consciousness. Appeals to mothering instincts, to women's values, to community service and charity—particularly when these were housed within and given the legitimacy of the church—allowed women of all different political orientations to act jointly in the social movements. In the short run, this was crucial to mobilizational success. In the longer run, the diversity of political views within the movements may have robbed them of an ideological cohesion necessary for sustained political activism.

Overall, then, gender appears to work in conjunction with religious personality to explain the limitations of partisan affiliation within these CEBs, at least.[29] Men and women of some religious orientations would be unlikely to be swayed by the CEBs' attempts at political consciousness-raising in any case, but for women the tendency to ignore or refrain from partisan activism is probably reinforced by gender stereotypes. Only a few exceptional women with a predisposition to liberationist consciousness-raising overcome this stereotype. In contrast, gender proved to be an important facilitator of the social movements, which, with a less clearly partisan agenda, could unite women of various political stripes behind common banners of motherhood and caregiving in a way that appeals to class consciousness could not. This, then, is one area in which the gender of participants may indeed have facilitated the CEBs' mission.

SIX

Liberation Theology and the Liberation of Women in Santo Antônio

Women have played a crucial role in the CEBs of Santo Antônio. This chapter looks at the other side of equation, asking what the Popular Church has offered women, and particularly whether the CEBs have contributed to their emancipation and gender consciousness. Historically, Catholicism and *marianismo* have been associated with patriarchal gender norms and women's exclusion from the public sphere in Brazil. Churches, however, can change, as the emergence of the Popular Church attests; moreover, as we have seen throughout, religious symbols and doctrines are sufficiently multifaceted and complex to allow a variety of interpretations. Finally, just as some elements of the CEBs, such as consciousness-raising and decentralized religious authority, potentially offer opportunities to change political consciousness, they may also inadvertently provide women the wherewithal to rethink gender consciousness. In fact, because religion seems to be intimately connected with attitudes toward gender and family, religious groups may even have a greater influence on gender consciousness than they have on political consciousness (Heaton and Cornwall 1989, 285).

Neither liberation theology nor the CEBs seek to transform patriarchy. Their primary mission is religious, and women join them from religious, not feminist, motives. Yet the Popular Church's potential for empowering women should not be dismissed out of hand: even religious groups with overtly discriminatory norms and practices can provide women with resources for combating subordination and breaking out of traditional roles (Lawless 1988a; Lawless 1988b; Kaufman 1985). The extent to which women are able to find such resources must be assessed, not assumed.

The liberationist church remains embedded in a religious structure that continues to discriminate against women in many ways and to oppose some policies that Western feminists deem indispensable to women's emancipation, such as legalized abortion and divorce. At the same time the CEBs themselves have encouraged women to break into new roles and particularly to empower themselves as citizens. Given this fundamental ambiguity, assessments of the CEBs' impact on women have varied, depending in part on what issues the analyst chooses to focus on. Focusing on women's new religious and public sphere roles, liberationists and their adherents conclude that the groups encourage gender equality and role-breaking (Goldsmit and Sweeney 1988; Golden 1991). In contrast, feminist scholar Sonia Alvarez contends that, despite having contributed to women's empowerment as citizens, the Popular Church stymies the development of gender consciousness around private sphere oppression and related feminist issues such as sexuality and reproduction (Alvarez 1990, 1991a, 1991b).[1]

Ultimately this debate may remain unresolved, since the same evidence leads to different conclusions depending on how a particular vision of feminism or women's liberation leads one to weigh gains in one sphere of life against those in another. Moreover, it reflects different perspectives on the significance of traditional gender roles, particularly motherhood, for women. Alvarez and other feminists like her see such roles as inherently constricting, reinforcing passivity and women's marginalization.[2] It is also possible, however, that poor women retain their allegiance to the domestic roles around which so much of their lives and identities revolve while transforming the roles in significant ways. Does "motherhood" reinforce *marianismo* and marginalization when it becomes an impetus for political action—a public rather than an exclusively private identity?

This chapter will suggest that at least for a minority of participants, such a transformation of traditional female identity is occurring. First, it is necessary to progress much further in specifying the opportunities and limitations of the CEBs regarding gender roles. In addition, we need to evaluate systematically the CEBs' impact on women's attitudes and their behavior in both the public and the private sphere. Finally, by exploring the response to CEB opportunities for raising gender consciousness, we may be able to identify conditions and characteristics that permit women to take advantage of such opportunities.

THE POTENTIAL FOR CULTURAL CHANGE:
NEW IDEAS AND NEW ROLES FOR WOMEN IN THE CEBS

Feminist scholars and others interested in religion's impact on gender roles describe a variety of ways in which religions affect perceptions of a society's gender system. Overt teachings about what constitutes a moral and well-constructed family, as well as about sexuality and reproduction more generally, are only the most obvious ways that religion shapes views on gender. Religious symbolism, imagery, and language—worship of a male deity, ambiguous female symbols like Eve, use of the universal male form in worship services—all can carry implied messages about women's relative worth and inclusion in a religious community (Christ 1982; Schneiders 1983). Hierarchical religious organizations that exclude women from important ranks can also contribute to their delegitimization as authority figures more generally.[3]

These sources of influence on gender ideology can be grouped into two categories: ideas and organizational structures. Assessing the CEBs' potential as a source for changing gender ideology requires first specifying the mechanisms through which they might foster such change. What specific and implicit new ideas do they offer members about family and about women's worth? What opportunities do they offer women to act on terms of equality with men or as bearers of religious authority?

Ideas about Gender in the CEBs

Liberation theology and the Popular Church offer relatively few overt teachings regarding private sphere issues like family and gender roles. This neglect led participants at the Fourth Ecumenical Meeting of Theology from the Woman's Point of View, held in São Paulo in 1992, to criticize liberation theology for reflecting class conflict, but not "the domination of one gender and of nature" (*Latinamerica Press*, April 30, 1992, p. 7). As feminist theologian Ivone Gebara points out, many women initially identified with liberation theology, but subsequently, beginning around 1985, began to develop their own theology to address "gender oppression, which is not addressed in liberation theology." Male liberation theology, she adds, is "another product of patriarchy" (*Latinamerica Press*, April 30, 1992, p. 7).

CEBs do focus on large political, class issues, while leaving domestic issues to groups like the *Pastoral Familiar* (Family Pastoral), which specializes in family and prenuptial counseling (Padilha 1982, 197–98). In Santo Antônio, the *Pastoral Familiar* sponsored workshops and weekend retreats for married couples. Although these were open to CEB members, the groups did little to promote them and few members were even aware of them. None of the active CEB members had ever participated in them. In general, the *Pastoral Familiar* seemed to be associated with a more conservative sector of the church and to be advertised through the more traditional parishes.

It is impossible though to avoid family issues when consciousness-raising sessions try to relate to the daily life of the poor. Women in the Mothers' Club discussions, for example, often talked about problems such as alcoholism, drug abuse, and unemployment, all of which affect family life for the poor in the urban periphery. These discussions usually remained at an abstract, impersonal level: "so many women" out there must deal with alcoholic or absent husbands, the participants would note. Although everyone knew that some women in the group had the same problems, their specific cases were discreetly avoided, left for one-on-one conversations with close friends after the meeting.[4] Moreover, when such issues did crop up, they were generally placed in the context of "the problems of the poor," a context that politicizes them and relates them to the CEBs' larger political and social goals. Thus, the solution for domestic problems according to the CEBs is engaging in social activism to change the oppressive structure of society. Women receive little guidance or comfort about their daily roles and personal lives (Mariz 1989).

Individual pastoral agents sometimes broach subjects relating to gender equality. Despite liberation theology's evolution toward a vague advocacy of equality for women, their position on such issues is highly individual. Madeleine Adriance describes a liberationist priest in rural Northeastern Brazil counseling men to share domestic responsibilities so their wives can have a more equal chance to participate outside the home (1993). In contrast, Sister Gabriela, a long-time CEB and women's group organizer in Itaim Paulista, related the problems of several more active women members whose husbands were both oppressive and abusive. Teresa felt forced to curtail her participation because of her husband's anger, and asked Gabriela: "Oh, sister, what can I do? I want two things: I want to participate, and I want to stay with Pascoal." Gabriela found this a moving testimony of Teresa's dedication to family and believes women must find a way to participate and yet maintain traditional values—even if they are being mistreated (field notes, Oct. 1986).

Between these extremes is Padre Chico who played a criti-cal role in the CEBs in Santo Antônio. While he rarely dis-cussed gender roles or family issues himself, Padre Chico en-couraged women in the CEBs to form groups to discuss their problems *as women*, not just as poor people. Moreover, he enabled a middle-class feminist organization, Rede Mulher, to meet and work with the Mothers' Clubs in the region. Rede Mulher, in turn, encouraged the women to discuss at least some issues related to gender equality and women's rights. Padre Chico seems to have been exceptional, however: mem-bers of the women's pastoral group in the region complained that male and female pastoral agents were more interested in mobilizing them to carry out tasks for the church than facili-tating their reflection on their situation as women (field notes, Oct. 1986). Women leaders in Chile expressed a similar sense that the church was more interested in mobilizing their labor now because it needs it, but that the creation of new roles for women and so on was not meant to promote gender equality or a rethinking of roles (Gilfeather 1977, 45).

The Popular Church has rarely questioned official church doctrine on issues such as divorce and abortion. Rede Mulher activists complained that pastoral agents sometimes cut off their attempts to discuss such issues (field notes, June 1986).[5] More generally, the CEBs tend to politicize these issues in class terms, much as they do issues like alcoholism. Pamphlets on birth control, for example, portray it as an imperialist plot and an oppressive burden on poor women. They want many children, the argument goes, and could have as many as they desired if resources were distributed more fairly.

More recently, theologians like Ivone Gebara have chal-lenged some of these ideas and begun to develop a specifically feminist liberation theology. Gebara has even called legalizing abortion a means of reducing "violence against life," a remark for which she was censured and silenced by her order (*Latin-*

america Press, Nov. 25, 1993, p. 4). Male theologians generally have not gone so far, although Leonardo Boff has declared that he see no insurmountable obstacles to women's ordination (Sigmund 1990, 84). Most have also increasingly recognized women—like blacks, Indians, and others—as a particularly marginalized group within the working class. The Second Feminist Encounter for Latin America and the Caribbean saw this response as insufficient. It included a workshop on "Patriarchy and the Church" that challenged liberation theologians to address the structures of patriarchy rather than just adding women as one more marginalized sector of the working class (Van den Eykel 1986, 315).

By the mid-1980s, five to ten years after feminist interpretations were arising in theological circles, little had trickled down to the base communities. In fact, with all of the reinterpretation of religious symbolism that the liberationists produced, there was virtually no liberationist interpretation of the Virgin Mary, despite the powerful appeal that she as a symbol could be expected to have for women in the communities. When I asked CEB members whether they had ever reflected on the life of Mary, most could only recall traditional novenas, celebrations for the Month of Mary, and so on.[6] Several thought nontraditional reflections would be useful and inspiring (interviews, Apr., Aug., Oct. 1986). The CEBs had not actively encouraged a new symbolic interpretation of Mary, although a number of relevant works had already appeared in print.[7]

Besides neglecting family and symbolic issues, liberationists initially subordinated gender to class oppression. When women were brought into the analysis, it was usually in terms of what they could do to help in the class struggle rather than how they might improve their own lot as women. For example, a 1983 pastoral campaign dealing with street crime in São Paulo completely ignored the issue of sexual violence against women

(Alvarez 1990, 389). Similarly, the 1984 campaign addressed the specific ways in which youth, blacks, Indians, and other groups were marginalized within society. Although women were listed, the only "specific" oppression they seemed to suffer was the lack of resources to meet their families' needs. Their response in the liturgy was "We want to walk together, united and organized. We don't want space to walk alone. We want to walk together with all the marginalized people, with our husbands, and with all the other workers!" (Para que todos tenham vida, 23–24). In contrast, the other groups were urged to organize themselves for their own needs.

CEBs may not actively promote traditional gender roles, but they often subtly reinforce them. As Katherine Gilfeather noted in Chile, church language frequently places women in a "maternal frame" (Gilfeather 1977, 42). Rhetoric in the communities often reinforces the women's shared perception that they have "special roles" and "talents" springing from biological motherhood which could be used in the class struggle. The 1984 campaign is only one example. Sonia Alvarez argues that liberation theology has produced "essentialist" interpretations that "do not question the socially constrictive, exclusive identification of women with maternity and the family" (Alvarez 1990, 388). On gender issues, the Popular Church vacillates between silence and implicit support of traditional norms.

Nonetheless, the CEBs have challenged traditional patriarchal notions in at least one way: they have encouraged women's entry into and active participation in the public sphere. And while the rhetoric sometimes appeals to women's "special talents," at other times it calls upon them to assume a unisex notion of the duties of the "conscientized Christian." As primarily female audiences were told that conscientization requires public sphere action for social justice, new forms of public behavior were legitimized. The church called upon women to take on new and unaccustomed roles and sanctioned the appropriateness of doing so. By calling on men and women to act in the same way as Christians, the CEBs at least partially subvert the concepts of "Christian men" and "Christian women" as two groups with different duties and appropriate (public versus private) behaviors. Thus the ideal of the "conscientized Christian" implicitly breaks down existing gender distinctions regarding at least some forms of appropriate behavior, as well as offering women a rationale and legitimization for venturing into new roles and realms.

Perhaps at least equally important, the CEBs also emphasized the role of lay leadership in making decisions. Because the church has always called upon them for service, it has always framed women in a potentially active way. As Gilfeather points out, however, the model is one of "devoted service," implying a subservience in keeping with the traditional model of femininity (Gilfeather 1977, 42). In contrast, the CEBs in theory, and at least at times in practice, gave the laity, and by extension women, much more control over *how* they would serve.

Finally, it is worth noting changes in the roles of women religious that might affect the CEBs. Most women religious working with CEBs are not traditional nuns. They live in the communities, wear common dress, and work, sometimes even in factories or other typically working-class jobs (Nunes 1985). In Santo Antônio, the only nuns who could be considered "traditional" were those working at the school for deaf-mutes. The others were hardly the "irmãzinhas" ("little sisters") of a cloistered life. They shared fully in community life and supported themselves, although often at somewhat more bourgeois jobs such as office or hospital work. Their independent, active lives can be seen as presenting an alternative model for women, as both Nunes and Adriance Cousineau argue (Nunes 1985; Adriance 1993). At the same time though, as Sister Gabriela exemplified, women religious do not necessarily promote more progressive gender roles in their interactions with women in the CEBs.

New Religious and Public Sphere Roles

CEBs expect conscientized Christians to be not only social activists but also full participants in the groups' religious life. As a result, the CEBs open up a variety of new positions to the laity as the Catholic Church has done generally since the Second Vatican Council (Neitz 1993, 169). Since most positions are open to laity regardless of gender, CEBs have expanded religious roles for women significantly. A subtle message of gender equality is also transmitted by men and women serving together in a variety of religious roles.

Many of women's leadership opportunities continue to be in sex-segregated groups. Each CEB usually has a Mothers' Club, and women tend to dominate certain other groups as well, like the neighborhood prayer groups. These groups give women an opportunity to lead other women and to exercise and develop a variety of skills, including public speaking. Moreover, some women's groups, such as the Mothers' Clubs, can become important and even dominant actors within a CEB. The Mothers' Club often raises most of the community's funds, for example, and does much of the daily maintenance and organization for the church. In many communities, its members also run other organizations, particularly catechists' groups. As a result, membership and especially leadership in the Mothers' Club may confer a degree of status and power on a small group of women.

While sex-segregated groups offer some important opportunities, membership in mixed male-female groups sends the clearest message of gender equality. Women and men can participate on an equal footing in a variety of ways: as elected community leaders, as members of ministries such as the ministry of baptism, which offer classes and perform certain sacraments in the absence of the priest, and as leaders of the Sunday celebrations that the community conducts when the priest is unavailable to say mass. Women's religious authority does remain limited by the fact that they cannot be ordained. Even women religious can fulfill basically only the same functions as lay men. Thus, despite the CEBs' attempts at democratization, the groups' ultimate religious authorities—priests and the local bishop—continue to be male.

Finally, social movements offer one more opportunity for participation in sex-integrated groups. As noted above, men and women are equally called upon as conscientized Christians to be activists on behalf of social justice. This not only confers a degree of equality but also opens the possibility of new behaviors and forms of participation in public life for women. We have already begun to see in the previous chapter that the CEB was an important factor in motivating many women to take on new roles and participate politically when they had done so only marginally before.

Summary

The liberationist church does not set out explicitly to challenge patriarchy or to promote a feminist agenda. Despite the emergence of feminist theologians and the gradual recognition of women as a particularly marginalized subsector of the poor, the CEBs often remain silent on gender issues, subtly reinforce existing gender ideology, or politicize domestic issues on a class basis that obscures gender issues. The ambiguity of the groups' messages cannot be overlooked. The CEBs call women to greater participation and offer a number of new and prestigious roles within the church on an equal basis with men. Moreover, they encourage women's more active role within the public sphere, albeit the attendant rhetoric sometimes calls on them as Christians and sometimes stresses their special capacity for social activism as mothers. Overall, then, the groups do offer women some opportunities to rethink existing gender roles and to break into new roles, but do not provide a comprehensive or cohesive critique of patriarchy.

BREAKING ROLES AND CHANGING ATTITUDES:
FINDING A NEW BALANCE

New Roles

The CEBs have apparently had the least impact on women's private sphere roles. CEB members uniformly shared traditional domestic roles: nearly all were married, widowed, or separated, and all of those were mothers. The only exceptions were the two youngest women who still lived at home with their parents and could be expected to move into wife-and-mother roles in the future, and one woman in her thirties, Cíntia.

Cíntia's decision to remain unmarried in order to devote her energies to organizing workers and women within the church and the PT is unusual. It is also partly attributable to her experiences in the Popular Church, although not necessarily in the CEB per se. While she is active in the CEB, Cíntia was a member of the church's young workers' organization (JOC) as a teen and continues to put most of her efforts into the Workers' Pastoral (PO).

Cíntia is unique among the women in the CEBs. According to Sister Holly, a pastoral agent with many years' experience in the PO, Cíntia is much more typical of PO activists. Holly claims that only particularly self-confident, autonomous women become active in the male-dominated PO and notes that few of those who do so are married, although they are in their thirties and forties. They seem, she says, to choose activism rather than marriage as the main source of their identity. It may be, then, that the PO had a strong influence on Cíntia's unusual role choices as it seems to have had on many others, but there is little evidence that the CEB itself influenced her.

As for the women in more traditional roles, few describe significant changes in their family lives as a result of their CEB participation. At least, few describe any positive changes. For example, no one reported that her husband had taken on additional domestic work after she began more active participation, although a few women had recruited daughters to work more for them. On the contrary, many have suffered a deterioration in their domestic lives as a result of their activism. It is not uncommon for women like Teresa, described above, to suffer repercussions from their husbands and families as a result of their participation. One woman's husband locked her in the house to keep her out of the CEB; others are barely on speaking terms with their spouses as a result of disagreements over their participation. Only a few of the most active, like Iraci and Maria dos Anjos, appear to have reached an accommodation in which their husbands tolerate or support their activism. Iraci's husband even overcame his initial opposition to her overnight trips to Rio for CEB meetings (interview, Nov. 1986).[8]

Men more readily acquiesce to women's participation in purely religious activities. In fact, women's participation in new religious roles is widespread and cuts across all three religious types. The women in the CEBs were active in a variety of ministries, particularly baptism, and were often involved in the communities' liturgy groups. As a result, the Sunday celebrations and reflections are often led by women. Iracema and Zélia, for example, often lead the celebrations in their communities. Samaritan religionists Marli and Chica also frequently participate in leading the celebrations, as does traditional religionist Cristina. Other traditional women's participation is curtailed in part by age and lack of literacy. Margarita, for example, cannot participate in leading the celebration because she cannot read the printed pamphlets, although she does actively participate when the reflection is opened up for comments from the congregation. In fact, during several celebrations I attended, Mothers' Club members of all religious types were the most frequent participants in the reflection.

Similarly, women of all three religious types are involved in the community councils. One of the communities in Santo Antônio has a fifteen member council composed of eleven women and four men. Although liberationist Iracema was the council coordinator, other women members of the council included traditional religionists Margarita, Olinda, and Neide, and samaritan religionist Chica.[9]

In all of these religious roles, women are implicitly equals with men. They lead worship and distribute communion alongside men—or by themselves—and they plan the future of the community from positions to which they have been elected along with male peers. Although many of the women were active in lay organizations in the past, often these were all-female organizations or charitable organizations that conferred status but little power or authority. By stepping enthusiastically into the new religious positions offered by the CEB, the women are potentially taking a new step toward authority and equality among laity, at least, within the church.

Finally, many of the women of all types have broken into new, public sphere roles by becoming active in the social movements and, to a lesser extent, in electoral activities. In contrast to the pattern with religious involvement, however, chapter 5 described political activism as dominated by samaritan and liberationist women. When traditional women participated, they did so more selectively and often on their own terms—terms that challenged their accepted roles less than demonstrating or working at a polling place might. While only a minority of women have responded to the CEBs' efforts to recruit them into these new roles, it is still important to note that the CEB proved an effective channel for the more activist women to take on unaccustomed, public sphere roles.

While the women have experienced little change in their domestic roles, then, many have taken on new religious roles. Women of all types have also become politically active through the CEBs, although the samaritan and liberationist women have been the most active and most likely to take on more challenging public sphere roles. Even if we only focus on that minority (twelve of thirty women are politically active in an ongoing way), there is no doubt that the CEBs have facilitated women breaking into new roles. If we include the religious roles as well, it becomes clear that the CEBs have offered at least the potential for women to be recognized as equals with men and as authority figures, as well as helping them to learn a variety of new skills including public speaking and organizing.

Roles alone are only a partial indicator of the CEBs' impact on women's lives and gender consciousness. Changes in attitudes may precede or lag behind changes in roles. We saw in chapter 4, for example, that although the majority of the women in the CEBs could be considered "nontraditional" in having worked outside the home, most viewed paid employment as a necessary sacrifice on behalf of their family. The new role, in essence, is sustained and legitimized by very traditional beliefs about women's proper sphere. Chapter 5 indicated that something quite similar occurs with many of the women who participate in the social movements as well: for many, it represents an extension of their traditional roles and is justified by a continued belief in women's essential nature and role as caregiver and mother. Seen in this light, one might argue that for these women, the new forms of participation represent not a new consciousness, but rather a new duty placed on women as an extension of patriarchal ideologies. Thus, Sonia Alvarez, for example, argues that although the CEBs have empowered women as citizens, they have failed to empower them *as women* (Alvarez 1990). Her conclusion may be overly hasty and over-generalized. In fact, at least some women have experienced the first stirring of gender consciousness as a result of their activism in the CEBs.

Changing Gender Attitudes

Women in the CEBs rarely criticize social expectations that they will take on the roles of wife and mother. Indeed, their widespread rejection of the label "feminist" stems in part from their equation of the term with a desire on the part of women to be "like men"—and implicitly "just as bad" as men. For example, Cristina commented "I'm not in favor of the feminist movement, because here's what I think. . . . A 'liberated' woman, one who calls herself liberated, for me, is a woman who smokes, who drinks. Can those be the rights women want?" (Nov. 1986). Cristina is a traditional religionist and one of the strongest advocates of traditional roles for women, but nearly all women of all religious types echoed her sentiment. For liberationist Iraci, for instance, feminism is misguided in placing too much emphasis on women's sexuality and sexual pleasure (Nov. 1986). Others commented that liberated women only wanted more sexual freedom "like men have."

Catarina alone willingly claimed the feminist label. She is the woman who took a job, despite her husband's objections, largely to liberate herself after eighteen years in "an oppressive marriage." Before joining the CEB, she had also started drinking and smoking in what she now regards as a misguided attempt at liberation. Catarina's attitudes antedate her CEB activism, but some of the difficulties she has experienced and sees other women experiencing since she joined the CEB reinforce her analysis. She shares her criticisms of marriage and men with the other women in a deliberate attempt to raise their consciousness.

In a milieu obsessed with capitalism and class relations, Catarina is the only woman who compares gender and class. Drawing a parallel between *machismo* in the home and capitalism in society, she remarked: "The "big people"—in this case, the men—aren't going to change a situation that only brings them privileges" (field notes, Dec. 1986). It is this oppression at home that women must fight in order to participate in the bigger social struggle, she said. She offered her own case as an example, saying, "Now I go where I want, and it's not that my husband doesn't object. He cares, but I don't care if he does. So eventually he'll stop bothering because it's not worth it" (field notes, Dec. 1986). Catarina has achieved only a minimal accommodation with her husband, who remains quite angry over her job and CEB participation.

Other very active, politically-involved women who have experienced many of the same difficulties at home express shock when Catarina compares male domination to capitalist domination.[10] Their rejection of feminism—and of Catarina's position—is based on their continued commitment to the private sphere. They eschew "feminism" because they equate it with a philosophy that is anti-family and anti-male. Even a simple proposal to carry a banner supporting "women's rights" provoked a furor in a Mothers' Club meeting because some participants saw it as sounding "like they were better than men" (field notes, Oct. 1986).[11] Whatever difficulties they may experience in their own lives, most women are shocked at the idea of conflict between men and women, and most continue (like Teresa) to value even a difficult and oppressive family life.

The women's widespread opposition to abortion, birth control, and divorce may reflect not only their religious upbringing, but also this generalized commitment to and valuing of domestic roles. Women of all three religious types were especially opposed to abortion and divorce. Opinion was more mixed about birth control, with some women of each type expressing the sentiment that birth control "nowadays" is acceptable. Many have daughters or daughters-in-law who use birth control, and the older women often applauded the decision as a sensible one. The women's major reservations about birth control, in fact, were medical rather than moral: most had heard stories of women who became ill from using birth control and feared the consequences for younger women.

By some North American standards of feminism, then, women in the CEBs could hardly be called feminists and don't accept that label themselves. They have by and large not given up traditional notions of women's "respectability" and proper roles. They do, however, express varying degrees of aspiration for a change in the balance of the male-female division of labor. The degree to which they desire to see a change in that division seems partly to be related to the extent to which they have taken on new roles. As their activism in the CEBs and social movements has increased, bringing them new roles and new responsibilities, women have been forced into an awareness that their changing roles have generally not been accompanied by a change in *men's* behavior and attitudes.

Women in the CEBs, as a result, have come to realize that they face implicit discrimination of various sorts. In fact, N. Patrick Peritore found that one characteristic of "liberationist" respondents in his survey was some statement of the view that the church discriminates against women (Peritore 1990, 146). For example, despite the fact that women now serve equally with men in authoritative religious roles, women realize that they are not as respected in these roles. Women of all religious types and pastoral agents commented that male attendance in the CEBs dropped off as women took on more religious roles. The women realize that men do not think they have moral or religious authority to lead worship services; they don't want to sit in church to listen to a "bunch of women" (field notes, Oct. 1986). As Iracema said:

> The ones who carry the community forward are women. Just last week we were discussing this, preparing the liturgy. We started to talk and we found that, particularly in our community here, it's the women who carry it forward. Then we thought, "Lots of people will feel that we are trying to be priests, because we've been assuming all the [religious] tasks." But I protest at that, because it's women who do all the work. Why is it that when it's time for a religious celebration, only men can be up there? (Apr. 1986)

Even men's acceptance of women religious is minimal. One sister complained that the bishop would prefer one bad priest to several dedicated sisters simply because men will not go to a mass led by women (field notes, Oct. 1986).

Since women of all three types take on new religious roles, at least some in each category express an awareness of the extent to which men reject their new authority. The more a woman participates, however, and the more extensively she does so outside as well as within the church, the more she is likely to come to realize that even if she is nominally "free" to take on the new roles, in practical terms it is impossible to do so without male cooperation.

Many traditional women, like Margarita, Cristina, and Neide, respond to the idea that the social movements are a new form of charity work—a means by which they can do good for others, especially children. They see their participation as an extension of their traditional womanly and religious roles. Margarita and Neide, especially, see no conflict between new and old roles. Both have extremely conservative ideas about women's domestic roles: Neide, for example, does not approve of working mothers and even contends that most poor women don't *have* to work but are merely trying to "get out of the house" and away from their responsibilities (field notes, Sept. 1986). With no small children and limited participation, Margarita and Neide are able to balance old and new roles without conflict and without modifying their gender ideology. They are critical of women who cannot.

Other traditional and samaritan religionists also criticize women who tilt the balance "too far" in the direction of new roles. At one Mothers' Club meeting, a number of women commented with dismay on the story of a young couple from another community. The woman participated a great deal in the CEB, and the couple was experiencing marital problems. Several women clearly blamed the wife, and one even wondered if "that was what she learned in all those meetings" (field notes, Oct. 1986).

Many traditional women believe uncritically that it is the wife's responsibility to make things right in the home. If that means curtailing her religious or social activism, so be it. Since they view that activism primarily as an extension of those traditional female roles anyway, curtailing it to harmonize with the more fundamental duties toward husband and children only makes sense. From this perspective, participation is not a woman's right, and a man has no responsibility to help her participate even when her activism is arguably improving conditions for the whole community, including him.

Some traditional and samaritan women, in contrast, have adopted a discourse that at least superficially challenges established gender roles. In fact, aside from Neide and Margarita, there is a fair degree of expressed unanimity that women's work is undervalued and that men and women should share household tasks more equally, especially when both work. Traditional religionists Cristina and Eloisa, for example, criticize men for not helping around the house when their wives work and for their preconception that it is unacceptable for men to do housework (interviews, Oct., Nov. 1986). Maria Angela also believes men and women should share domestic responsibilities more equally (Nov. 1986). Liberationist religionist Iraci said she would have remained single if she had been *conscientizada* earlier because women's domestic roles and men's refusal to help around the house limit her participation too much (Nov. 1986).

There is a difference between these expressions and those of other liberationist and some samaritan women. While nearly everyone thought gender roles ought to change a bit with men "helping out" more around the house, few women described this change as a necessary step toward real equality for women. Moreover, many of the traditional and samaritan religionists continued to have such an extensive notion of what women's domestic responsibilities entail that they could not possibly carry them out and participate more than marginally in the new religious or social roles the CEBs offer. Maria Angela, for example, gave a detailed account of women's responsibilities toward their husbands and children, while declaring that women could take on all kinds of public responsibilities. It seemed hard to imagine, however, that one could participate and live up to her expectations of domestic roles (Nov. 1986). Similarly, Cristina argued for a slightly more balanced division of labor, but at the same time in her own life she sees her commitment to being home with her children—and she stresses that it is their *mother* they need—as an obstacle to anything more than marginal participation, especially in social movements (Nov. 1986). Even liberationist Iraci, who recognizes the difficulties that an unequal division of labor has created for her own participation, argues that in the final analysis, it is the woman who must harmonize things at home. If her husband has not "accompanied" her conscientization and participation, then she is responsible for slowing down a bit to avoid problems (Nov. 1986).

Just as with the political discourse in the communities, then, caution is in order in interpreting the women's apparently consensus position that domestic male-female relations must change. In fact, only a small minority of mostly liberationist women argued strongly not just for "help," but for real *equality* and a division of labor that allows women to assume what they see as their *right* to participate. Joselina explicitly criticized the church's role in fostering the idea that married women should submit to their husbands through the inclusion of that injunction in the marriage ceremony. She added, "There's that idea, you must be submissive to the man, that was put in women's heads. . . . But it can't be that way. Because we have to be free too, we have to be something. Can it be that we think we're lowered, that the man is the head, we're not the head? But then, don't I have a head equal to his?" (Aug. 1986). She stressed that since men and women are now equal in many of their other roles, like work and social activism, they should be equal in the home as well. Young Célia also believed that women need to learn to question a patriarchal model of marriage and assert their right to equality (Oct. 1986).

Equality is especially important to these women because they see their participation outside the home as not just another religious or charitable activity—one that can be dispensed with if necessary—but rather as a right and something that has become necessary to their personal fulfillment. Many told their own stories or abstractly described women's yearning to break the isolation of household duties for a life in the larger world (Apr., Oct. 1986). Simone stated the case most strongly for the right to participate for one's own fulfillment as well as in service to others. When she became more active, her husband resented the loss of a model wife who kept a perfect house, but she says, "I was unhappy in those days. I was just an object, without my own life. Now I say to him, that's not why I was born. I was born to live, not to live for you" (Nov. 1986). Similarly, Zélia uses her former inability to participate in anything outside the house as the ultimate expression of how oppressed she was in her marriage. She adds that women "must have their rights, to study, to work, in the church, in politics. Everyone must see that she isn't an object, a toy. . . ." She also describes the real equality in domestic responsibilities between her son (a former priest) and his wife. They also participate equally in their community in Rio. Zélia sees this as the model of a marriage she would have liked to have had (interview and field notes, Oct. 1986).

Another liberationist, Maria dos Anjos, also linked the idea of domestic equality with women's rights outside the home:

> Liberation for women within the home is to be equal to the husband. . . . That's the liberation we want to create. Liberation for the woman to be free, for her to be free to go to a meeting, to have a right to earn and keep her salary, to have a right to do things without the husband telling her not to go. None of that! We're free. We're married, but not for him to oppress me: for the two of us to be equal. (Oct. 1986)

Samaritan religionist Fátima argues that "The liberation I see for us, for women, is equality." She adds, "Women can participate in everything, not just in work. We can participate in everything. Why do only men have a right to participate and not us? I think we should have equal rights" (Nov. 1986).

Comparing these comments with the discussion of participation in the last chapter, it is clear that women with the strongest views on equality and women's right to participate correlate closely with those who actually do participate most heavily in not only religious but also political activities. It is impossible to say whether their attitudes developed primarily as a result of their participation in the CEB. They may have been among the more autonomous and self-confident women to begin with; indeed, this might be suggested by the liberationists' penchant for seeing religion as a challenge. Moreover, they did have contact with the feminist group Rede Mulher through the CEB, and many attributed their ability to articulate what had only been vague feelings of discontent earlier to discussions with the feminist organizers. Nonetheless, the fact that these women were the ones who met with the feminists suggests that they already had some sense of their gender-specific problems.

At the very least the CEB provided the experiences that crystallized the first stirring of a critical attitude toward existing gender relations. The women who chose to participate most intensively are also the ones who, as a result, felt the clash of old and new roles and expectations most strongly. Simone left her husband in 1989 because he could not accept her increasing commitment to activism and her desire to work outside the home. Other women, like Iracema and Zélia, suffered criticism and virtual ostracism from their husbands for their participation. Iracema, in particular, receives no support from and is barely on speaking terms with her husband, who makes clear his resentment of her public role and the notoriety she has achieved in the community. Without the experience of new roles outside the home and the conflicts with domestic life that these created, it is doubtful that most of these women would have ever experienced such a strong rethinking of traditional gender roles.

The activist women can be seen as simultaneously preserving and transforming traditional aspects of feminine identity. They cling to motherhood, especially, as a source of special power and gratification for women. At the same time, they want to create a *political* rather than purely private role for maternity. They reject the image of the passive, submissive, and long-suffering mother in favor of a more public, active model.

This balancing of old and new interpretations of femininity is inherently tension-filled. Thus, the most active women experience not only familial problems but also a certain amount of anxiety. They do not want to abandon their family roles for self-fulfillment or sacrifice the family's well-being to that of the community, but neither do they want to curtail the activism they see as both a right and a responsibility. The only way they can reconcile the two, however, is for men to change their roles as well.

By continuing an ambiguous discourse that mingles biological essentialism with a call for women and men to be equals in participation and activism, the CEBs have in some respects only heightened the anxiety women experience. Moreover, the CEBs have been singularly incapable of changing most men's attitudes. A few women, like Maria dos Anjos, have husbands who are also active in the CEBs and who, they claim, appreciate and support their wives' activism as a result.[12] Most women reported that their husbands do not participate. Most do not even attend Sunday celebrations. As a result, they do not understand their wives' activities very well and have little incentive to change their own behavior in order to be more supportive.

Unless the church can reach men more effectively or can provide women with a space for developing a new discourse that will help them reconcile old and new roles to achieve a more feasible balance, it will have reached its limit in contributing to women's growing gender consciousness. While this has never been the church's objective and it would be unfair to criticize it on those grounds, it would potentially be in the interest of the Popular Church to pay more attention to this issue. The liberationist and more activist samaritan women in Itaim seem to have concluded that such a limit had been reached by the mid-1980s. They reacted in two ways. First, they have begun to push for a greater voice in the church. Many interviewees complained that while they do most of the work, they are denied access to decision-making roles above the community level. This sentiment appears to be widespread among women leaders throughout the archdiocese of São Paulo.[13] Since 1990, several women in Itaim have experienced significant rifts with the bishop over what they perceive as a disregard for their views (Drogus 1992, 82).

This led to the second reaction: the women formed an autonomous, secular group aimed at raising women's gender consciousness. In fact, as the women expected, dom Angélico was extremely wary of their organization and refused to give them a meeting place in the diocese's buildings, even though its organizers are key CEB leaders and the diocese allocates space to other secular groups. The women's group of the Zona Leste (AMZOL) still exists separately from the CEBs although the same women are active in both. It continues to try to organize and raise the consciousness of women on a variety of social issues and has increasingly moved on to specifically feminist topics including workshops on patriarchy and sexuality. Its leaders have attended Latin American regional feminist conferences.

CONCLUSIONS

The CEBs are primarily religious organizations with a secondary agenda that seeks to promote class consciousness. They are not intended to be feminist groups nor do women join them from feminist motivations. In fact, it is precisely their continuity with women's expected roles and with an established church that has reinforced patriarchal ideas of gender relations that attracts many women to them in the first place.

Neither the groups nor the women they attract begin with an expectation of changing cultural norms relating to gender. Moreover, despite their new theology and religious practice, the CEBs remain embedded in a Catholic Church that continues in many respects to promote traditional gender roles. Nonetheless, the CEBs also offer at least glimpses of opportunities for women to rethink their own worth, authority, and roles.

How have women responded to these opportunities? Is there evidence that the CEBs have somehow empowered women? Clearly Sonia Alvarez is correct to conclude that the CEBs have been most empowering for women in the public sphere. Even then, only a minority of women have become politically active on an ongoing basis. Most of the women have at least some experience of public activism now, however, and most likely none would have been active at all without the opportunities and encouragement presented by the CEBs. This is an important accomplishment and first step for these women, many of whom are middle-aged or older, with little education, and very traditional upbringing.

Alvarez is also right that less has changed in the domestic sphere. All of the women continue to fulfill—and for the most part, to cherish—their familial roles, a position that probably reflects a combination of sentiment and practicality.[14] Most continue to believe in women's "special" nature and roles. One could conclude from this, as Alvarez does, that they are trapped in a "constrictive" notion of female identity. To do so would be to miss the important transformations that have occurred, albeit unevenly, among the women in the CEBs.

For activist women, especially, subtle changes are taking place in their perceptions of and beliefs about gender. Although they remain committed to motherhood as a source of identity and strength, this starting point has led many of them into the public sphere. This is certainly a transformed notion of motherhood, one that identifies it with public activism rather than private passivity.[15] The activists who share this transformed concept of motherhood are similar to the

Mothers of the Plaza de Mayo in their insistence that "family" issues are also a matter for the private sphere and in their rejection of traditional models of submissiveness.

If women regard motherhood as producing only a new *duty* to act on behalf of others, it might mean little. In that case it is only another burden in the sexual division of labor, as so many women perceived work outside the home. While for some women it may have this meaning, the activist women, however, generally now regard public participation as their *right*. This constitutes an important transformation in their view of womanhood and its appropriate relationship to the public and private sphere. The phenomenon of women gaining greater confidence, authority, and an increasing conviction of their right to participate in religious and social life on equal terms seems to occur among women CEB leaders in countries as diverse as Brazil, Mexico, Chile, and Peru (Ferguson 1990).

Greater gender consciousness has not spread uniformly among women in the CEBs, just as class consciousness has not. What seems to distinguish the women who have embraced it more fervently is their level of activism and the consequent difficulties they experience at home. Not even all of the most active women make this leap: Iraci, for example, continued to be more similar to the traditional women in her views on gender, but seemed to have reached an accommodation with her husband that permitted her to participate. For other liberationist and samaritan women, the experience of domestic clashes combines with a firmer commitment that prohibits them from simply dropping their activism to produce the realization that their new roles require an adjustment in the old gendered division of labor.

The CEBs have not resolved this conflict—perhaps no institution could—because it inheres in the situation. Despite years of North American feminist organizing and theorizing, many women in the United States and Canada continue to express the same dilemma. The CEBs are particularly hampered by their difficulties in changing the behavior and attitudes of men, however: male congregants often leave rather than accept women's religious authority, and male family members often will not adopt new ways to support the women's participation. Moreover, the CEBs' discourse on gender is sufficiently ambiguous to leave the women torn between private and public sphere duties and rights.

The CEBs have produced neither a widespread gender consciousness nor a level of consciousness that many Western feminists would identify with. Indeed, whatever gains women have made have been largely an inadvertent byproduct of their participation rather than something with which the CEBs should be directly credited. But women, especially liberationist and samaritan women, have taken advantages of the opportunities and ambiguities in the CEBs to make significant gains and attitudinal changes. As W. E. Hewitt notes:

> women . . . are at the very least being provided with opportunities to take up leadership roles in both the Church and society. Certainly, the CEBs do not offer women total freedom to fulfill all their aspirations and achieve their full potential. But for those who are determined and persistent, much more can be accomplished than many feminist observers would admit. (Hewitt 1991, 66)

Women have taken on leadership roles, and the leaders, especially, have begun to rethink gender roles. With the support of middle class feminists—facilitated by local pastoral agents in this case—they have begun to organize themselves as women. Perhaps most importantly, although they cannot change their husbands' behavior, many are trying to change that of their sons and daughters. As a result, the women's experiences in the CEBs may produce the most discernible impact on gender roles and relations in the next generation.

SEVEN

Conclusions

Women, Religion, and Sociopolitical Change

In urban Brazil, the Popular Church is also in many areas primarily a women's church. Recognizing and analyzing the potential reciprocal impact of gender and religion in the *comunidades eclesiais de base* is important because it permits us to ask and answer a series of questions. We can address two important empirical questions: What difference does women's dominance make for the CEBs' project of social and political change? And what difference have the new religious groups made for gender relations? In other words, have women energized or stymied the Popular Church with its sociopolitical goals, and has the liberationist church in turn empowered women?

These empirical questions are important to understanding the functioning and the fate of the CEBs in Brazil, and, indeed, anywhere in Latin America where the groups have been dominated by women. The answers can also provide significant insight into larger theoretical questions. The experience of the liberationist church is but one instance of a global phenomenon in which religious elites seek to transform popular consciousness, both religious and political. Its fate, and an understanding of the factors that combined to produce it, illuminate both the difficulties facing such projects of religious transformation and the obstacles any ideological entrepreneurs are likely to encounter. In addition, looking at the CEBs' impact on gender attitudes and roles allows us to assess the debate over whether religion is a conservative force with respect to gender—a "bulwark" of patriarchal institutions and culture.

GENDER, CULTURE, AND RELIGION

The evidence from Santo Antônio suggests that poor women's lives are in many ways gendered. Their roles in a gender-based division of labor color the ways in which they experience urban poverty. They also share a culturally defined view of woman-hood and a belief in women's unique abilities—springing from their maternity—to perceive and rectify certain kinds of problems not only within the family but also in the community. These common experiences and beliefs provide a crucial connection among the women but do not translate into a singularly gendered religious worldview. In fact, women's religious personalities vary considerably, a fact reflected in their diverse responses to liberation theology. The most important shared aspect of their religiosity is their other-oriented value emphases—charity, love, and social justice. But while these emphases can be joined to an appealing feminine language related to family, children, and service when the CEBs make liberationist ideas concrete in the social movements, they are diverse enough in their political implications to thwart both partisan political projects and a thoroughgoing "conversion" to liberation theology.

This finding points to the fact that consciousness-raising "failed" in its efforts at relating a class-based interpretation of biblical symbols not because "women are too conservative," but more generally because the obstacles to translating a religious elite's new ideas into popular consciousness are overwhelming. For religious movements, in particular, one obstacle is the multifaceted nature of the religious symbols themselves: even if the priest calls Christ "liberator" rather than "savior," many facets of the symbol still resonate with older interpretations, and some individuals will continue to think in terms of individual salvation. Gender *may* play a partial role in this response: the proportions of religionists of various types may differ between men and women, but the evidence here cannot answer that question. In any case, communicating inherently complex, multifaceted symbols to people whose individual religious personalities are quite different means that at best, only some of the audience is likely to "hear" the message the elite means to convey. The Popular Church erred in thinking that the poor would eagerly respond to a class-based message, for not only gender, but other factors such as religious personality affect their response.[1]

IMPLICATIONS FOR SOCIAL AND POLITICAL CHANGE

This uneven change in consciousness suggests a very real limitation on the church's ability to generate social change. If people's ideas are not changing in a way that leads them to question political, economic, and social structures, and if they continue to await changes initiated from above, the long-term prospects for social change have been little affected by the CEBs' consciousness-raising efforts. Moreover, the heterogeneity of political attitudes among CEB members who were mobilized for social movements and other forms of political action in the 1970s and 1980s may provide one explanation for why these movements eventually evaporated and did not produce lasting changes in the form of partisan involvement or ongoing movements.

At the same time, however, the CEBs must be credited with at least a short term impact on political behavior. Most importantly, they successfully mobilized a previously politically marginal group—poor women—in movements for social change. Despite the short-lived character of most of these movements, their real impact on poor neighborhoods in the form of schools and health posts built, roads paved, and street-lights installed, should not be underestimated. Their efforts seem dwarfed by the magnitude of the problems in the Zona Leste, but the movements produced concrete improvements for the lives of many residents.

Their ability to produce such changes brings us back to the question of gender. While gender alone probably was not the main barrier to raising class consciousness—since changes along those lines correspond to religious personality—it does appear to have had a contradictory effect on the CEBs' attempts at political mobilization. Gender may be at least partially accountable for the CEBs' apparent inability to generate much enthusiasm for what women regard as "dirty," competitive, male-dominated party politics generally and PT activism in particular. At the same time, however, gender seems to have provided the glue necessary to hold a social movement of people with divergent political beliefs together. Women in the CEBs were able to use their common gender roles and beliefs to mobilize large numbers in support of family and neighborhood issues that *combine* class and gender. A class-based mobilizational strategy alone would have been unlikely to attract as many women, particularly from among the traditional and samaritan religionists.

Santo Antônio's CEBs, like other female-dominated social movements throughout Latin America, illustrate that women are not necessarily excluded from the public sphere by their gender roles, culture, or religion. They are not inherently more conservative than men. They can become catalysts for social change. In fact, the very things that were once thought to make them conservative—domesticity, church attendance, a cultural norm of submissiveness and self-abnegation—can under the right circumstances become an impetus for their involvement in movements for social change. The Popular Church should be credited with providing circumstances that helped to mobilize women as a short-term, but nonetheless important, force for change, proving that it, too, is not inherently conservative.

Even if we refute the assumption that women and religion equal conservatism, we must admit the political limitations of both. Women's activism in Santo Antônio, for example, throws light on the debate between North American feminists such as Jean Elshtain and Mary Dietz over the implications of mobilizing women for political activism along gendered lines. Elshtain maintains that women can and should be mobilized in defense of family and life-related issues, while Dietz claims that only if women stop thinking like mothers and start thinking like citizens can their political activism be effective (Elshtain 1982; Dietz 1985). The experience of women's movements in the CEBs suggests that Elshtain is right about the way to maximize political involvement by women. However, the fact that only those minority liberationist women who began thinking along more "political" and less "maternal" lines continued to engage politically in movement and partisan politics suggests that Dietz's insight with respect to long-term political involvement is correct.

Similarly, a religious movement's ability to generate long-term involvement and social change is probably inversely proportional to the extent to which it maintains a strictly moral posture. Moral exhortations and utopian depictions of future polities that leave much room for individuals to reinterpret in line with their own religious and political bents can be extremely effective short-term mobilizers. Without engaging in and developing a real political program, however, such moralism is likely only to result in mobilizing opposition on a short-term basis.

Despite the very real limitations of the CEBs' ability to generate lasting political involvement and profound political change, they have produced local leaders in many poor communities. Most impressively, they have fostered the development of women's leadership abilities. Such leaders are not pervasive, but they can achieve important objectives and their example may be important for future generations. The new example of women's political activism, especially, may be a source of changing role models whose full impact will only be seen as a younger generation of women comes of political age.

THE CHURCH AND CHANGING GENDER ROLES

Some feminists contend that public involvement like that promoted by the CEBs "inevitably" produces gender consciousness, if only the "constrictive" church would not preempt women's attempts to rethink gender roles. But women vary in the degree to which such activism produces a feminist consciousness, and this variability occurs among women in the same CEBs. It is at least as attributable to their different personalities and degrees of politicization as to the church's attempts to squelch rising gender consciousness. Given their value emphasis, for example, traditional women in the CEBs are unlikely to develop a gender consciousness under any circumstances and would probably be particularly unreceptive of attempts at feminist proselytizing.

In contrast, the church-based movements, despite their limitations, have led almost all of the women some distance toward rethinking gender roles and identifying ways in which they are discriminated against as women. Their response to this discovery varies with their level of political involvement (and thus conflict with traditional roles) and their religious personality: liberationist leaders are the most likely to recognize and react against the limitations that society and the church place on them as women.

More perhaps cannot fairly be expected from a movement with no feminist agenda. The opportunities the Popular Church has provided women are limited, but they are real opportunities, and many women have seized them even to the extent of moving outside the church to broaden their scope for feminist discussion in secular groups, like AMZOL.[2] Others have at least thought—perhaps for the first time—about inequalities in their domestic lives even if they have not become "feminists." Moreover, it is unclear how much such emerging feminist consciousness can do in the absence of larger social, structural changes. For poor women, as long as opportunities for education, employment, and economic independence remain restricted, marriage and family will continue to be their most practical and attractive options. It may be, however, that this generation of women leaders, with their increasing consciousness of the tension between public and private roles, will help their children to forge new, more equitable family structures in the future. Certainly many are consciously trying to do so, as a result of their own experiences and frustrations with the contradictory gender ideology of the CEBs.

WOMEN'S PARTICIPATION AND FUTURE OF THE POPULAR CHURCH

Women played crucial roles in fostering the growth and organizing the social movements of the Popular Church. Now, women's participation also increasingly poses a challenge to the church. Feminist theology questions some of the church's fundamental teachings, including those on abortion and an all-male clergy. The emergence of women leaders who are increasingly critical of the church's seeming inability to help them reconcile their private and public roles or encourage men to modify their own behavior poses another problem. So far the church in Brazil has tended to ignore these women and has done little to facilitate their search for answers to their problems. But given the critical role that such women play in the day-to-day life of the CEBs, the church ignores them at its peril. Liberationist women, especially, are already inclined to question the institutional church, and the self-confidence that the CEBs have helped foster only increases this tendency. The women themselves recognize, although the church may not, that they constitute its main labor force. They are willing to question and be selective about their "devoted service," if not to withdraw from the church altogether (Gilfeather 1977, 42).

The Popular Church has thus potentially set centrifugal forces in motion through the CEBs. Conservative bishops are right to fear that the consciousness-raising, democratization, and decentralization of power in the CEBs could lead them to question the authority of the hierarchy. Traditional and samaritan religionists are not likely to join in this challenge. They—especially traditional women—are also unlikely to be tempted to defect to the growing Pentecostal community. The church is thus unlikely to lose all of its female base of religious activists, but it does stand in danger of losing its female leadership as activists, if not as communicants.

THEORETICAL LESSONS AND FUTURE DIRECTIONS

What lessons from this case can be applied more broadly to inform future studies and develop theory? First, much more theoretical and empirical work needs to be done on the relationship between gender and religiosity.[3] It has too frequently been assumed that there is a direct, monocausal relationship between gender and religion, whether the assumption is that women are traditional or that they are more like liberationists. This study suggests that gender may produce certain similarities in the kinds of religious and value themes that appeal to women, but beyond that, they interpret these themes in very different ways. Family, charity, neighborly love, and social justice may all be other-oriented themes, but they have very different political connotations and implications. In the future, more research would be useful to sort out the varieties of women's religious personalities and possibly to identify other sources of difference. In addition, work comparing men's and women's religious attitudes would help to establish precisely what aspects of religious personality are gendered.

Second, with respect to gender roles and religion, the study confirms that religion can play an active role in reinforcing or changing gender stereotypes, and that it sometimes does so unintentionally. The feminist critique of religion as a mainstay of patriarchy is at best partially correct: institutional, mainline Christian religions rarely set out intentionally to promote a feminist agenda. Nonetheless, it is important to recognize the variety of ways in which religions may present opportunities for women to rethink and develop new gender roles. As with political consciousness-raising, women's receptiveness to these opportunities varies, and establishing what makes some women seize available opportunities and others reject them would be an important contribution to understanding the force of religious ideas in society.

Finally, this case underscores that religion can be a catalyst as well as an obstacle to social and political change. To understand how much change a religious movement generates and why, we need to look not only at the ideas it intentionally promotes, but also at how those ideas are received by the faithful.[4] If we can also pinpoint what accounts for those responses— gender, religious personality, other demographic factors, institutional or other organizational factors—we can begin to understand *why* people have acted on certain religious ideas politically, and why they have often acted in unexpected ways. In the CEBs, for example, mobilization for social movements was less a sign of widespread success at liberationist consciousness-raising than an indication that local leaders had managed to unify people with divergent political views around vague moral, religious, and gender-related themes. Understanding the real nature of their political activism makes the subsequent political trajectory of the CEBs more comprehensible.

WOMEN MAKING HISTORY: WOMEN, RELIGION, AND SOCIOPOLITICAL CHANGE

The story of women in Santo Antônio's CEBs can be used to serve many analytical and theoretical purposes. The purpose that Iracema, Zélia, Adelita, Simone and others hoped it would serve was to show those outside Brazil that poor, religious Brazilian women are not passive victims. They can, and do, participate in making their own history. They realize that they cannot always make it just as they please, but their faith and determination prevent them from giving up. Inside or outside the Catholic Church and the CEBs, they intend to continue trying to change conditions for the poor, and increasingly, for poor women in particular.

These poor women also do not necessarily think or behave in just the ways that politicians, religious leaders, or North American or Brazilian feminists would like. This is not surprising, since in contrast to their critics and would-be mentors, they operate in the complex interstices of class and gender, radical and traditional ideas and beliefs. Their contribution and their shortcoming has been to patch these ideas together in ways that produce movements for change that appeal to people, especially women, of varied beliefs or various "levels of consciousness." Such movements may be unlikely to produce revolutionary change, but they can begin and contribute to the long, slow process of changing culture and generating better conditions for the poor and for women.

Notes

ONE.   POPULAR CHURCH, WOMEN'S CHURCH

1. Translation mine.

2. See especially the classic work, Mecham 1966.

3. On Latin American Catholicism's role in reinforcing gender inequality, see especially, Stevens 1973; Safa 1979; Saffioti 1979; and Goldsmit and Sweeney 1988. Molyneux argues that the church was a conservative brake on women's mobilization in Nicaragua.

4. Miguel Concha M., Oscar Gonzalez G., Lino F. Salas, and Jean-Pierre Bastian, *La participacion de los cristianos en el proceso popular de la liberación en México (1968–1983)* (Mexico City: Siglo Veintiuno Editores, 1986), 30. Quoted in Ferguson 1990, 181. Translation by Catherine Ferguson.

5. For example, Vallier 1972b; Hobsbawm 1959.

6. This history is described more fully in chapter 2.

7. Daniel Levine has been the single most important social scientist leading research in this direction.

8. Important exceptions are Gilfeather 1977 and 1985; see also Flora 1975 for an important comparison of Catholic and Pentecostal women.

9. Most recent books on the Popular Church devote a few pages to gender issues, while the most important edited volume on the women's movement in Latin America mentions the church on only a handful of pages in two chapters. Among recent books, Burdick 1993, Levine 1992, and Hewitt 1991 consider gender as a factor, but other volumes such as Ireland 1991 and Keogh, ed., 1990 are generally silent on the topic. Jaquette, ed., 1991 mentions the church's role in the women's movement only in articles by Sonia Alvarez (Brazil) and Maruja Barrig (Peru).

Testimonial literature such as Golden 1991 provides some first-hand accounts of women's experiences with the Popular Church, but little social science analysis.

10. See Levine 1991 and 1992, as well as his earlier works.

11. A 1994 nationwide survey of Brazil found women to be the majority of all Catholic subgroups, except "traditional Catholics" which were 52.9 percent male. In fact, women outnumbered men in all other non-Catholic religious groups as well (Pierucci and Prandi 1995, 29).

12. Van den Hoogen cites examples from throughout the region as well as from other Catholic cultures in Van den Hoogen 1990, 172.

13. Again, this type of qualitatively different experience also seems to be characteristic of the Mediterranean Catholic cultures.

14. The community also implicitly recognizes the fact that women may suffer from particular patterns of neglect and abuse based on gender. They point out that women may suffer guilt when their husbands, not knowing whom else to blame, blame them for lack of food, and that women may suffer physical abuse by husbands (Golden 1991, 41).

15. For examples of research on religiosity utilizing these categories, see Benson and Williams 1986; Welch and Leege 1988; and Leege and Welch 1989.

16. See, for example, Heaton and Cornwall 1989; Brinkerhoff and MacKie 1984, 1985.

17. See, for example, Spretnak 1982. More comprehensive lists of these critiques can be found in Heaton and Cornwall 1989, and Brinkerhoff and MacKie 1985.

18. Hewitt (1991, 63) briefly notes this perspective. It was also common among some pastoral workers in São Paulo, especially men, who perceived the base communities as hopelessly traditional and conservative precisely because they were composed of women who "only wanted to pray."

19. In a twist on Alvarez's contention about leadership roles, John Burdick claims that the church has offered only unrealistic and limited options to women to improve their situations.

20. The 48 percent figure is more recent than the others and is from Pierucci and Prandi (1994, 32). In Brazil, the "minimum salary" is set by the government and is commonly used for accounting and sociodemographic comparisons. A single "mini-

mum salary" is not a minimum in the sense that it is sufficient to support an individual or family. Five minimum salaries are often used as a "poverty line" measure.

21. Again, this is to reinforce the "critical case" nature of the study.

TWO. "THE MIDWIVES WERE WOMEN"

1. As W. E. Hewitt points out, some proponents of the "grassroots" interpretation of the origins of the Popular Church, such as Otto Maduro, describe it as a fairly spontaneous creation of the popular classes. Most scholars, however, emphasize the institutional church's role in its creation, even if, like Mainwaring, Adriance, or Hewitt himself, they also believe that the laity and CEBs played a role in shaping the final outcome. On this debate, see Hewitt 1989.

2. Some women now figure in the list of theologians as well, as discussed in chapter 6. Their writings are relatively recent, however. They were not formative for the liberationist church, and they also remain relatively marginalized.

3. By preconciliar, I mean the church before the Second Vatican Council (1962–65), whose ideological and liturgical changes opened the way for the liberationists' innovations.

4. In addition to writings by liberation theologians themselves (Gutiérrez 1973; Segundo 1976; Boff 1982; Boff and Boff 1984, 1987), those wishing more background on liberation theology specifically will find Berryman (1987) especially useful.

5. See especially chapter 2 of Levine (1992) for a general discussion of the Popular Church in the region. Excellent descriptions of the emergence of the liberationist church in Brazil include Mainwaring (1986), Adriance (1986), and chapter 1 of Hewitt (1991). See also Hewitt (1989) for an evaluation of contending theories regarding the sources of the church's option for the poor in Brazil.

6. On this point, see Hewitt (1989, 1991), Mainwaring (1986), and Levine (1992).

7. See Adriance (1986, 58–60) and Mainwaring (1986, 108) for descriptions of the emergence of the first groups resembling the organizational and pastoral form of CEBs.

8. CEBs as an organizational form, however, are not inherently linked to liberation theology. As Levine points out, CEBs

can be used for quite conservative purposes, and they vary greatly in the extent to which they take on a liberationist aspect. This is true not only across countries in the region, but also within the same national church (Levine 1992). Despite liberationist predominance in Brazil in the 1970s, many members of the hierarchy opposed the option for the poor. These bishops either discouraged CEB formation or attempted to develop communities without liberationist content. Bruneau and Hewitt (1989) discuss the differences across dioceses in Brazil.

9. Levine (1992) equates the liberation theology-CEB relationship with that between theory and practice.

10. On the roots of liberation theology, see Dorr 1983.

11. For a description of the Brazilian context, see Hewitt (1991, 14). Levine describes similar patterns throughout Latin America and considers them essential to understanding the rise of the Popular Church throughout the region (Levine 1992). See also chapter one of Berryman (1987). Articles by Poulat, Levine, Hebblethwaite, and Houtart in Keogh (1990) provide important discussions of the regional and international context shaping the emergence of the liberationist church. Burdick (1993, chap. 2) provides an excellent overview of contrasts in different types of Catholicism, including preconciliar and liberationist.

12. Indeed, liberation theologian Leonardo Boff considers the literacy movement, with its emphasis on consciousness-raising, to have been a critical moment in the radicalization of Brazilian Catholic thought (Boff 1984b: 22; Bruneau 1974: 80). See De Kadt (1970) for a detailed account of the organization of peasants and its accompanying literacy movement, the *Movimento de Educação de Base*. He describes particularly the participation of university students.

13. See also Levine (1992, 35). Berryman (1987, 15–17) also offers a useful summary of Vatican II's importance.

14. The first prominent liberation theologian, Peruvian Gustavo Gutiérrez, was an advisor at Medellín (Berryman 1987, 24).

15. Pierucci and Prandi found that CEB members were disproportionately drawn from the poor, although not the very poorest sectors of Brazilian society (Pierucci and Prandi 1995).

16. Mainwaring considers the Brazilians pioneers in developing liberationist-oriented CEBs as a new pastoral form (Mainwaring 1986, 146). Daniel Levine sees them as exemplars of the

sociocultural transformation ideal, which is liberationist but less explicitly interested in class conflict and politicization than the radical ideal (Levine 1992, 48).

17. My characterization of dom Angélico and the tone of the diocesan documents is supported not only by opinion within the archdiocese but also by observations in Hewitt 1986, 184–86.

18. Figures for the diocese from dom Angélico's office; for the parish, from the parish office. It should be noted that because CEBs, unlike parishes, do not have legal status, the diocese can only estimate their numbers.

19. One exception to this generalized statement should be noted. The parish supports a school for the deaf which is managed by a group of Italian nuns of the Providência para Surdos e Mudos. These nuns have very little direct contact with the CEBs, although individually CEB members may help at the school. In recent years, moreover, Padre Angelo appears to have become disenchanted with the radical line of the younger pastoral agents in the parish, and he has withdrawn from the CEBs to concentrate much of his effort on the school.

20. Adriance concurs that most CEBs are initiated by a visit from a priest or nun, so her predominantly rural sample shows the same pattern as this urban one (Adriance 1991, 299).

21. For comparison with the activities of CEBs throughout São Paulo, see Hewitt (1991, 69).

22. Women from other communities independently expressed the same conviction (field notes, Aug., July 1986).

23. Given Pierucci and Prandi's national figure of 54–60 percent women, it seems likely that rural CEBs are more gender balanced than those in São Paulo (Pierucci and Prandi 1995).

24. This conclusion is suggested by the figures on gender from Pierucci and Prandi (1995) which also show above average concentrations of self-identified CEB members in more rural states and lower than average CEB identification in urban São Paulo and Rio.

THREE.   BEING POOR, BEING FEMALE

1. See, for example, Betto 1981.

2. This study suffers from a number of flaws, including a high percentage of responses that were "uninterpretable," but the

preponderance of rural and urban peripheral CEBs has not been disputed.

3. São Miguel Paulista is not only a neighborhood next to Itaim, but also (as here) the name of an administrative district that includes Itaim. (Itaim Paulista, however, is a distinct electoral district, so although most socioeconomic data refer to the administrative district, figures on voting are for Itaim Paulista specifically.)

4. The sources of this difference are unclear. It may reflect the fact that Itaim Paulista's growth has been somewhat faster and more recent than that of São Paulo's periphery generally, so that Hewitt's numbers may actually be closer to the proportion of migrants in the population of the periphery as a whole. In that case, migration would not appear to distinguish CEB members from other residents of the periphery. It may also reflect the fact the Santo Antônio sample's focus is on active *women,* who tend to be adult women over twenty, an age group that is much more heavily composed of migrants than the under-twenty age group (see Caldeira 1984, 88). Had more youths been included, the proportion of migrants would have diminished.

5. One couple of Italian and Greek descent were born in Egypt and migrated to Brazil as adults.

6. A few described themselves as from "small towns." One woman grew up in Ilhéus (BA).

7. For example, Aug., Oct., Dec. 1986.

8. Cecilia Mariz makes this point with respect to CEBs in northeastern Brazil (Mariz 1994). See also Mariz (1989, 91).

9. At the time of the interviews most women in Santo Antônio were middle-aged and had lived in the city for an average of nineteen and a half years. A wider survey of women in CEB Mothers' Clubs throughout the eastern and southern periphery of São Paulo found similarly that the women were not the most recent arrivals in the city: on average they had lived in São Paulo over twenty-five years (calculated based on information provided by Rede Mulher). Their respondents had lived an average of 25.7 years in São Paulo. Since Rede Mulher's study focused on women in Mothers' Clubs, their respondents were slightly older: 42.4 years on average, versus 37.8 years for the women in Santo Antônio. The current study included several younger women who are CEB members but are not in the Mothers' Clubs. Their

relative youth also influenced the statistic on length of time in São Paulo.

10. See also Petrini (1984, 49).

11. Interviews, Sept. 1986 (Itaim), Sept. 1986 (Ipiranga), and Apr. 1986 (Osasco).

12. I report this information despite serious flaws in Ricco's research because, while it may be inaccurate in particular details, the general trend it indicates is supported by other research.

13. Pentecostals were much more disproportionately drawn from the ranks of the very poor than CEB members.

14. These figures represent Hewitt's findings for "L-CEBs," the group most socioeconomically similar to those in Santo Antônio. A full explanation of the *salário mínimo* or minimum salary is contained in note 20, chapter 1.

15. While I use the present tense for this aggregate data, I should point out that some of the women are widows, and this statistic includes occupations of their deceased husbands. Thus, one of the small business men, for example, sold meat at the *feira* in a small town in Bahia. His wife moved to São Paulo upon his death to join children in the city.

16. This figure compares well with a larger sample of women from CEBs in the Zona Leste which found that 66 percent were housewives and 33 percent worked outside the home. These figures are based on my own calculations from personal data gathered and recorded by Rede Mulher in 1985. This unpublished data was made available to me at their office.

17. Caldeira (1984) describes the process by which migrants gradually construct and expand their homes in a neighboring area of São Paulo's periphery.

18. Since the initial interviews, a daughter-in-law and granddaughter have also moved in while one son has moved to "the city."

19. The argument that Catholicism's practice and teachings have contributed to the subordination of women has been often made and need not be repeated in detail here. For examples from Brazil, see Morais (1985, 38), and, especially, Saffioti (1979, 90–105). Molyneux also argues that the church was a conservative brake on women's mobilization in Nicaragua (1985, 243).

20. At this point, we must also add a caveat. While official church pronouncements and some aspects of popular religious

devotion certainly seem to strengthen the cultural emphasis on women's identification with the private sphere, like all religious symbols, Mary is subject to a variety of interpretations by people of faith. Moreover, contrary to the assumptions of many critics of the Catholic Church's male hierarchy, women, particularly poor women, have often gained their only access to important public roles and prestige through the church. They could gain recognition as *beatas* and *sacristãs,* respected individuals who fulfilled certain religious functions such leading devotional prayer (Myscofski 1985, 50–51).

21. Hahner makes this point with respect to women of the popular classes in nineteenth-century Brazil as well (Hahner 1990).

22. This figure almost exactly duplicates Hewitt's finding that 58.3 percent of CEB members were married (1985, 120).

23. Rede Mulher's study of women's groups in the Zona Leste also indicated an average of 3.4 children per woman.

24. To residents of Itaim, downtown São Paulo is "the city." Although largely urbanized, Itaim is still clearly peripheral to the older and wealthier central neighborhoods. The Camargos, located on the edge of the metropolitan area, are still somewhat rural: people manage to keep small livestock in their yards and there is more open space nearby. Caldeira notes similarly that residents of Jardim das Camélias in São Miguel refer to downtown as "São Paulo" (1984, 119).

25. Since the completion of this study, the east-west metro line has expanded, but as the line runs south of Itaim proper, this still means a bus trip of thirty to forty minutes.

26. See Caldeira (1984, 59–62) for a discussion of the impact of transportation on daily life in neighboring São Miguel Paulista. In São Miguel, closer to the central city than Itaim, workers who earn up to five minimum salaries spend an average of 3.22 hours a day in transit.

27. A pastoral worker with long experience with the PO remarked that women in the PO—considered a "men's" pastoral—are very "individuated and autonomous." She states that, like Cíntia, most are unlikely to marry and seem to have established their identity primarily in terms of their work and their commitment to organizing workers (interview, Sept. 1986).

28. These "maternal feminists" are often regarded with suspicion as disguised neoconservatives by other schools of feminism.

29. Her husband's identification of their own situation with the Thatchers' was made particularly clear by his sympathetic portrayal of Mr. Thatcher. Seu Waldemar said that people may not say anything to Dennis Thatcher's face, but he must realize that "the other men are making fun of him behind his back when he goes down to the bar for a drink."

FOUR.   EACH IN HER OWN WAY

1. Rolim (1980a, 108) and Petrini (1984, 37–38) support the idea that behavior, especially mass attendance, separates popular Catholics from the more orthodox.

2. Petrini (ibid.), Rolim (1980b, 52–53), and Cleary (1985, 108) also imply that CEBs recruit among folk Catholics.

3. Berryman (1973) argues that CEBs are likely to alienate folk Catholics whose spirituality is oriented toward the miraculous. Sanks and Smith (1977) describe Chilean CEBs as having enormous difficulties reaching folk Catholics. Studies in São Paulo and elsewhere in Brazil also conclude that CEB members seem mostly to be drawn from those who are already frequent church attendees. See Burdick (1993), Hewitt (1991), and Bruneau (1987).

4. A similar story was recounted in my interview, Oct. 1986.

5. The quotation is from an interview conducted by Rede Mulher in 1984, but the same story was repeated to me by the respondent in an interview, July 1986. Interview, Nov. 1986, also described going to mass in Guaianases when she first moved to São Paulo from Ceará.

6. The youthful desire to be a nun was also expressed by another respondent in an interview, May 1990.

7. Interviews, July, Sept., Oct. 1986.

8. Other information from interviews, Apr., Oct., Nov. 1986, and field notes, July 1986. Hewitt confirms the importance of pastoral agents in inspiring and bringing together a CEB.

9. Many North American sociologists of religion recognize the necessity of looking at various dimensions of "religiousness" which are not necessarily interconnected. See, for example,

Benson and Williams (1982); Leege and Welch (1989); and Welch and Leege (1988).

10. This group also has many similarities to the type Cristián Parker calls "justice" Christians (Ferguson 1990, 120–22).

11. This group is quite similar to Parker's traditional Catholics (Ferguson 1990, 119). Parker identifies such people as popular sector Catholics but not CEB members. John Burdick, however, describes two very similar groups and says that they do participate in the CEBs (Burdick 1993, 185, 188).

12. Similar to Parker's "renewed traditional believer" (Ferguson 1990, 119), this group is like the category Burdick found in a CEB on the periphery of Rio, whom he characterizes as equating "liberation as self-reliance" (Burdick 1993, 187–88).

13. Only Cleide and Eliane, the two young women who are irregular mass attendees, seem closer to the "nominal" religious type: less interested in and able to comment on religious themes, these nominal religionists tend to participate in religious groups primarily for social reasons. Cleide, for example, stressed that she participates if people invite her, while Eliane wanted to participate to get out of the house and have a social life (interviews, June, Aug. 1986). Both participate more in activities such as craft classes and church bazaars than in strictly religious services or activities. Francisca, who also participates irregularly, practices Afro-Brazilian religion and may also be best described as a nominal CEB member.

14. In fact, they are the only type for whom challenge is a highly emphasized theme, according to Benson and Williams.

15. This is from an interview with an activist in Itaim who has since moved from the area, conducted by Rede Mulher (1984).

16. One exception is Catarina, who has the lowest level of commitment to the institutional church of any of the women. Despite a background of orthodox attendance, she now considers herself "not much given to praying" and is minimally involved in her community in specifically religious activities. Her vision of God is also unorthodox: she said only that she believes "in some kind of force, a superior intelligence" (interview, Sept. 1986). The combination of extremely low pro-church attitudes, a symbolic vision of God, and a value emphasis on justice indicates that she is the only "nontraditional" religionist in the group.

17. Interviews, Oct. 1986.

18. The same comment was made by a pastoral agent in Ermelindo Matarazzo (interview, Oct. 1986) and in an interview with a group of nuns working with CEBs in the northern periphery of São Paulo (interview, May 1986).

19. Interviews, Aug., Sept., Oct., Nov. 1986.

20. Interview, Oct. 1986.

21. Field notes, Sept. 1986. Interestingly, she does not believe that capitalism breaks up families or forces women to work in Brazil.

22. Interviews, Nov. and Oct. 1986; field notes, May 1986.

23. Note the similarities with Burdick's respondent, Carlita: "helping others. We in the church have always done this. We must give bread to the hungry, clothing to the naked, visits to the sick . . ."(Burdick 1993, 186).

24. Interview, Nov. 1986. Tiradentes was a leader of a failed republican movement, the Inconfidência Mineira, in 1789.

25. In a 1988 sample, the number increased to 77 percent, but as the number of members had also decreased, Hewitt is skeptical as to the significance of this change (Hewitt 1991).

26. See Levine 1992 and Fleet 1992.

27. While I do not have systematic interview evidence on the relatively small number of active men, I did observe their interactions with the women in a variety of settings and often spoke with them informally. A thorough survey would be needed to substantiate this impressionistic conclusion, but it should also be noted that others (Burdick 1993, Levine 1992) cite examples of men who are closer to the traditional or integrated religionists here.

FIVE.   TIES THAT BIND

1. The president-elect, Tancredo Neves of the opposition party, died before taking office. The first civilian president was his vice-presidential candidate, José Sarney, who had been a member of the pro-military party.

2. On these points, see chapter 2, as well as Burdick (1993, 1).

3. For examples, see Gutiérrez (1979, 1–2); L. Boff (1984b, 9) and L. and C. Boff (1984, 91).

4. The anthropological study reported in Caldeira (1984 and 1986–87) is particularly useful for comparing "conscientized" and "unconscientized" attitudes because it was carried out in São Miguel Paulista, a region bordering on and socioeconomically similar to Itaim Paulista. It focused on the types of political attitudes and activities at issue in this chapter. Finally, it included several individuals who participated in a local CEB.

5. Benson and Williams concluded from their North American sample that liberationist (people-concerned) religionists tended to hold liberal political beliefs, while traditional (self-concerned) religionists are politically conservative (Benson and Williams 1986).

6. Two of Caldeira's respondents, also active CEB members, were among those who expressed the conviction that rich and poor need each other (1984, 152, 160).

7. Cleide did speak of the rights of the poor, but interestingly, she saw these as deriving from the taxes they pay (interview, Aug. 1986). In contrast, liberationist religionists had a less legalistic notion of rights.

8. On a different occasion she repeated this idea, saying that workers must vote for workers, because the owners only defend their own interests which are not those of workers (field notes, Oct. 1986).

9. Samaritan religionist Marli also says workers' and bosses' interests are opposed, and this is why the bosses do not want the workers to have a say in politics (interview, Nov. 1986).

10. The tentative, hypothetical quality of these statements is particularly clear in the Portuguese since they were often stated in the past subjunctive (which denotes an event not expected to occur).

11. The liberationist religionist was Maria dos Anjos (interview, Oct, 1986).

12. Interviews, Sept., Oct., Nov. 1986.

13. Interviews, Aug., Oct., Nov. 1986.

14. In nearly the same words, she and Simone also expressed the conviction that no individual can really be "free" or "at peace" "while there are poor children who are hungry" (interviews, Sept., Dec. 1986).

15. Exceptions included the younger women, whose participation in the CEBs began prior to their reaching political ma-

turity. Zélia, a liberationist religionist, recalled that because of her family background she had always discussed and been interested in politics, but claimed that she still had not participated much (interview, Oct. 1986).

16. An interviewee in another area of São Miguel also said that she had always simply voted the way her husband told her to, until she joined the CEB (interview, July 1986).

17. Similarly, Hewitt found that 55.6 percent of lower-class CEB members said that their "consciousness of social and political problems" was enhanced by participation in the CEB (1985, 129).

18. Field notes, Aug., Sept. 1986.

19. The possibilities grassroots groups hold for psychological empowerment of the poor have been stressed by Sara Evans and Harry C. Boyte. For examples from grassroots groups in the United States, see Evans and Boyte (1986), and Boyte and Riessman, eds. (1986).

20. The phrase *a união do povo* is so pervasive in the CEBs that it is frequently stripped of all political meaning. When one member of Comunidade São Francisco invited his neighbors over for a *feijoada*, for example, he described the party as a good example of *a união do povo*.

21. As reported in *Latin America Regional Report: Brazil,* Sept. 14, 1989:3.

22. See Della Cava (1989, 156–57) and Gómez de Souza (1982, 708–9).

23. Galletta describes the emergence of the 113 tendency which includes trade unionists, "independent intellectuals," and representatives of the church (Galletta et al. 1986, 43).

24. Bruneau (1987), Bruneau and Hewitt (1989), and Hewitt (1991).

25. Except for Neide with regard to the PT specifically.

26. Indeed, a rather hot discussion arose between pro-PT Iracema and anti-PT Conceição over the gubernatorial candidate, Eduardo Matarazzo Suplicy. Conceição pointed out that he was hardly a worker as the PT propagandists liked to claim, since he is a cousin of the Matarazzos, one of Brazil's great industrial families. Having worked in a Matarazzo textile mill, she didn't think much of the family's pro-worker credentials. Iracema suggested that Suplicy was from the "poor branch" of the family and didn't

have much money himself (field notes, Sept. 1986). Similar discussions occurred from time to time about whether or not Lula really did have a big house in São Bernardo.

27. This conclusion is shared by a Rede Mulher activist with several years of experience working in the communities of Santo Antônio and Itaim Paulista (interview, Nov. 1986).

28. This interview took place in a different parish in the same diocese, but I believe that the presence of pastoral agents is of equal importance for the more traditional women in all CEBs.

29. Elsewhere, this would certainly be only a small part of the explanation. Many CEBs did not take as strong a partisan stance as those in Itaim and Santo Antônio.

SIX. LIBERATION THEOLOGY AND THE LIBERATION OF WOMEN IN SANTO ANTÙNIO

1. See Hewitt (1991, 63) for an excellent summary of this debate.

2. For a feminist critique of the Mothers of the Plaza de Mayo that is similar to Alvarez's critique of women in the CEBs, see María del Carmen Feijóo (1991).

3. More comprehensive lists of these critiques can be found in Heaton and Cornwall (1989) and Brinkerhoff and MacKie (1985).

4. Burdick also noted that women in the CEBs he studied outside Rio de Janeiro felt very uncomfortable and unsupported when they tried to bring up personal problems (Burdick 1990, 1993).

5. Hewitt reports a similar case in which pastoral agents inhibited discussions in a women's group led by one of their own CEB organizers (Hewitt 1991, 65).

6. Two, Iracema and Maria dos Anjos, recalled having read, on their own time, books that portrayed Mary as a poor woman and an activist. They both felt that these books had an important impact on their formation as activists.

7. For example, Mesters, 1977; L. Boff 1979b, 1980.

8. Adriance (1993) claims that CEBs have transformed men's as well as women's roles, and that women generally feel their husbands support their activism. This evidence should be interpreted cautiously, however, since it is based on a onetime in-

terview. Most women in Santo Antônio initially claimed in formal interviews that their husbands supported them, although they "had heard of" cases where men did not. Only more repeated interactions and observations resulted in women spontaneously volunteering the fact that relations with their husbands had been strained by their CEB activism.

9. Women generally are well-represented on the councils, according to W. E. Hewitt. In 1984, 63 percent of council members in his São Paulo sample were women. In 1988, 46 percent were women. Among groups with no council, he found that men and women were about equally represented in authority positions (1991, 64).

10. When Catarina made these statements, the pastoral agent present, Sister Neide, also seemed shocked and tried to refocus Catarina's remarks in a more class-oriented vein.

11. Interestingly, it was a long time before anyone came up with a slogan dealing with women's issues at all in a meeting planning a rally for "Women and the New Constitution." Most proposed either vague slogans about land reform or workers' rights. The first idea to refer to women was Marli's "More respect as women." It was the inclusion of the idea of *rights* by Iracema that provoked an argument.

12. Adriance (1993, 15) reports that active husbands do change their roles in ways that promote greater domestic equality in rural CEBs in Northeastern Brazil.

13. This interpretation is based on unpublished transcripts of interviews conducted by Rede Mulher in 1984 and 1985. I am grateful for access to this material.

14. The alternative, of course, is separation or divorce, which leaves a poor woman in particular quite economically vulnerable. It would be surprising if many rushed to embrace this option.

15. Marguerite Bouvard Guzman makes a similar argument regarding the Mothers of the Plaza de Mayo (Bouvard 1994, 184, 187–88).

SEVEN.   CONCLUSIONS

1. John Burdick does not explore the issue of religious personality, but suggests that other demographic factors, such as

race and age, also influence who among the "poor" is likely to embrace or reject the liberationist church. He concludes that its appeal is inherently limited (Burdick 1993).

2. Hewitt (1991) also contends that feminist scholars have generally underestimated the degree to which the CEBs have fostered women leaders in particular.

3. Mary Jo Neitz cites the need for continued research on "how religious experiences and structures are gendered" and for that research to draw on theoretical developments in other areas of sociology, such as other aspects of feminist theory (Nietz 1993, 177).

4. Daniel Levine has been the major proponent of this point (see 1986b, 1989, and 1992).

References

Adriance, Madeleine. 1986. *Opting for the poor: Brazilian Catholicism in transition.* Kansas City: Sheed and Ward.

———. 1991. Agents of change: The roles of priests, sisters, and lay workers in the grassroots Catholic Church in Brazil. *Journal for the Scientific Study of Religion* 30: 292–305.

———. 1993. Daughters of Judith: Feminist consciousness in rural base communities in Brazil. Paper presented at the annual meeting of the Society for the Scientific Study of Religion, Raleigh, N.C., 29–31 October.

Allport, Gordon W. 1973. The religious context of prejudice. In *Research in religious behavior: Selected readings,* edited by B. Beit-Hallahmi, 82–103. Monterey, Calif.: Brooks/Cole Publishing.

Alvarez, Sonia. 1990. Women's participation in the Brazilian 'People's Church': A critical appraisal. *Feminist Studies* 16, no. 2: 381–408.

———. 1991a. *Engendering democracy in Brazil: Women's movements in transition politics.* Princeton: Princeton University Press.

———. 1991b. Women's movements and gender politics in the Brazilian transition. In *The women's movement in Latin America: feminism and the transition to democracy,* edited by Jane Jaquette, 18–71. Boulder, Colo.: Westview Press.

Avelar, Lúcia Mercês de. 1985. O Voto feminino no Brasil. Ph.D. diss., Pontífica Universidade Católica-São Paulo.

Azzi, Riolando. 1977. A Igreja católica no Brasil no período de 1950 a 1975. *Religião e Sociedade* 2 (November): 79–109.

———. 1984. A Participação da mulher na vida da igreja do Brasil (1870–1920). In *A mulher pobre na história da igreja Latino-americana,* 94–123. São Paulo: Ediçoes Paulinas.

Bakan, David. 1966. *The duality of human existence*. Chicago: Rand McNally.

Barreiro, Alvaro. 1982. *Basic ecclesial communities: The evangelization of the poor*, translated by Barbara Campbell. Maryknoll, N.Y.: Orbis Press.

Batson, C. Daniel and W. Larry Ventis. 1982. *The religious experience: A social-psychological perspective*. New York: Oxford University Press.

Benson, Peter L. and Dorothy L. Williams. 1982. *Religion on Capitol Hill: Myths and realities*. New York: Oxford University Press.

Bernardino, Angélico S. 1984. A Igreja dos pobres, sinal do reino de Deus. In *Fé e participação social*, 81–90. São Paulo: Edições Paulinas.

Berryman, Phillip. 1973. Latin American liberation theology. *Theological Studies* 34, no. 3: 357–95.

————. 1980. What happened at Puebla. In *Churches and politics in Latin America*, edited by Daniel H. Levine, 55–86. Beverly Hills: Sage.

————. 1987. *Liberation theology*. New York: Pantheon Books.

Betto, Frei (Alberto Libânio). 1981. *O que é comunidade eclesial de base*. São Paulo: Brasiliense.

————. 1983a. As comunidades eclesiais de base como potencial de transformação da sociedade brasileira. *Revista Eclesiástica Brasileira* 43, no. 171: 494–503.

————. 1983b. God bursts forth in the experience of life. In *The idols of death and the God of life*, Pablo Richards et. al., 159–64. Maryknoll, N.Y.: Orbis.

————. 1986. *Cristianismo e Marxismo*. Petrópolis: Vozes.

Boff, Clodovis. 1983. Crônica teológica do V° encontro intereclesial de comunidades de base (Canindé CE, 4–8 July 1983). *Revista Eclesiástica Brasileira* 43, no. 171: 471–93.

————. 1984. *Agente de pastoral e povo*. Petrópolis: Vozes.

Boff, Leonardo. 1979a. Christ's liberation via oppression: An attempt at theological construction from the standpoint of Latin America. In *Frontiers of theology in Latin America*, edited by R. Gibellini, 100–132. Maryknoll, N.Y.: Orbis.

————. 1979b. *O rosto materno de Deus: Ensaio interdisciplinar sobre o feminino e suas formas religiosas*. Petrópolis: Vozes.

————. 1980. *A ave-Maria: O feminino e o Espírito Santo*. Petrópolis: Vozes.

————. 1982. *Jesus Christ liberator: A critical christology for our time.* Maryknoll, N.Y.: Orbis.

————. 1983. CEBs: A igreja inteira na base. *Revista Eclesiástica Brasileira* 43, no. 171: 459–70.

————. 1984a. *Como pregar a cruz hoje numa sociedade de crucificados.* Petrópolis: Vozes.

————. 1984b. *Do lugar do pobre.* 2d ed. Petrópolis: Vozes.

————. 1986a. *A fé na periferia do mundo.* Petrópolis: Vozes.

————. 1986b. *E a igreja se fez povo—Eclesiogênese: A igreja que nasce da fé do povo.* 2d ed. Petrópolis: Vozes.

Boff, Leonardo and Clodovis Boff. 1984. *Salvation and liberation: In search of a balance between faith and politics.* Maryknoll, N.Y.: Orbis.

————. 1985. *Teologia da libertação no debate atual.* Petrópolis: Vozes.

————. 1987. *Introducing liberation theology,* translated by Paul Burns. Maryknoll, N.Y.: Orbis.

Bourque, Susan and Jean Grossholtz. 1984. Politics as unnatural practice: Political science looks at female participation. In *Women and the public sphere,* edited by Janet Siltanen and Michelle Stanworth, pp. 103–21. New York: St. Martin's Press.

Bouvard, Marguerite Guzman. 1994. *Revolutionizing motherhood: The mothers of the Plaza de Mayo.* Wilmington, Del.: Scholarly Resources Books.

Boyte, Harry C. and Frank Reissman, eds. 1986. *The new populism: The politics of empowerment.* Philadelphia: Temple University Press.

Briggs, Sheila. 1987. Women and religion. In *Analyzing gender: A handbook of social science research,* edited by Beth B. Hess and Myra Marx Ferree, 408–41. Beverly Hills, Calif.: Sage.

Brinkerhoff, Merlin B. and Marlene M. MacKie. 1984. Religious denominations' impact upon gender attitudes: Some methodological implications. *Review of Religious Research* 24, no. 4: 365–78.

————. 1985. Religion and gender: A comparison of Canadian and American student attitudes. *Journal of Marriage and the Family* 47: 415–30.

Bruneau, Thomas. 1974. *The Political transformation of the Brazilian Catholic Church.* Cambridge: Cambridge University Press.

————. 1982. *The church in Brazil: The politics of religion.* Austin: University of Texas Press.

————. 1987. Brazil: The Catholic Church and basic Christian communities. In *Religion and political conflict in Latin America,* edited by D. Levine, 106–23. Chapel Hill: UNC Press.

Bruneau, Thomas C. and W. E. Hewitt. 1989. Patterns of church influence in Brazil's political transition. *Comparative Politics* 22, no. 1 (October): 39–61.

Brusco, Elizabeth. 1986. The household basis of evangelical religion and the reformation of machismo in Colombia. Ph.D. diss., City University of New York.

————. 1993. The reformation of machismo: Asceticism and masculinity among Colombian evangelicals. In *Rethinking Protestantism in Latin America,* ed. Virginia Garrard-Burnett and David Stoll, 143–58. Philadelphia: Temple University Press.

Burdick, John. 1990. Gossip and secrecy: Women's articulation of domestic conflict in three religions of urban Brazil. *Sociological Analysis* 50, no. 2, 153–70.

————. 1992. Rethinking the study of social movements: The case of Christian base communities in Brazil. In *The making of social movements in Latin America: Identity, strategy, and democracy,* edited by Sonia Alvarez and Adolfo Escobar, 171–84. Boulder, Colo.: Westview Press.

————. 1993. *Looking for God in Brazil: The progressive Catholic Church in Brazil's urban religious arena.* Berkeley: University of California Press.

Caldeira, Teresa P. R. 1984. *A política dos outros: O cotidiano dos moradores da periferia e o que pensam do poder e dos poderosos.* São Paulo: Brasiliense.

————. 1986–87. Electoral struggles in a neighborhood on the periphery of São Paulo. *Politics and Society* 15, no. 1: 43–66.

Campbell, Ena. 1982. The Virgin of Guadalupe and the female self-image: A Mexican case history. In *Mother worship: Theme and variations,* edited by James J. Preston, 5–24. Chapel Hill: University of North Carolina Press.

Christ, Carol. 1982. Why women need the goddess: Phenomenological, psychological and political reflections. In *The politics of women's spirituality: Essays on the rise of spiritual power within the feminist movement,* edited by Charlene Spretnak, 71–86. Garden City: Anchor Press.

Cleary, Edward L. 1985. *Crisis and change: The church in Latin America today.* Maryknoll, N.Y.: Orbis.

da Matta, Roberto. 1991. *Carnivals, rogues and heroes: An interpretation of the Brazilian dilemma,* translated by John Drury. Notre Dame, Ind.: University of Notre Dame Press.

Davidman, Lynn and Arthur L. Greil. 1994. Gender and the experience of conversion: The case of 'returnees' to modern Orthodox Judaism. In *Gender and religion,* edited by William H. Swatos, Jr., 95–112. New Brunswick: Transaction Publishers.

De Kadt, Emanuel. 1967. Religion, the church and social change in Brazil. In *The politics of conformity in Latin America,* edited by Claudio Veliz, 192–220. New York: Oxford University Press.

———. 1970. *Catholic radicals in Brazil.* London: Oxford University Press.

Della Cava, Ralph. 1989. The 'People's Church,' the Vatican, and abertura. In *Democratizing Brazil: Problems of transition and consolidation,* edited by Alfred Stepan, 143–67. New York: Oxford University Press.

Demo, Pedro and Elizeu Calsing. 1981. Reflexões sociológicas: Relatório da pesquisa sobre CEBs. In *Comunidades: Igreja na base,* 13–64. 4th ed. São Paulo: Paulinas.

Dietz, Mary. 1985. Citizenship with a feminist face: The problem with maternal thinking. *Political theory* (February): 19–37.

Doimo, Ana Maria. 1984. *Movimento social urbano, Igreja e participação popular.* Petrópolis: Vozes.

Drogus, Carol Ann. 1988. We are women making history: Political participation in São Paulo's CEBs. Discussion paper no. 81. University of Wisconsin-Milwaukee Center for Latin America.

———. 1990. Reconstructing the feminine: Women in São Paulo's CEBs. *Archives de sciences sociales des religions* 71: 63–74.

———. 1991. Religion, gender, and political culture: Attitudes and participation in Brazilian basic Christian communities. Ph.D. diss., University of Wisconsin-Madison.

———. 1992. Popular movements and the limits of political mobilization at the grassroots in Brazil. In *Conflict and com-*

petition: *The Latin American Church in a changing environ-ment,* ed. Hannah Stewart-Gambino and Edward Cleary. Boulder, Colo.: Lynne Rienner.

Elshtain, Jean. Antigone's daughters. *Democracy* 2, no. 2: 46–59.

Escobar, Arturo. 1992. Culture, economics, and politics in Latin American social movement theory and research. In *The making of social movements in Latin America,* edited by Arturo Escobar and Sonia Alvarez, 62–88. Boulder, Colo.: West-view Press.

Evans, Sara and Harry C. Boyte. 1986. *Free spaces: The sources of democratic change in America.* New York: Harper and Row.

Feijóo, Maria del Carmen. 1991. The challenge of constructing civilian peace: Women and democracy in Argentina. In *The women's movement in Latin America: Feminism and the transition to democracy,* edited by Jane Jaquette, 72–94. (1st ed.) Boulder: Westview.

Ferguson, Catherine. 1990. The poor in politics: Social change and basic church communities in Santiago, Lima, and Mexico City. Ph.D. Diss., University of Denver.

Fleet, Michael. 1982. Christian communities in Chile and Peru. Working paper no. 183, Helen Kellogg Institute for International Studies, University of Notre Dame.

Flora, Cornelia Butler. 1975. Pentecostal women in Colombia: Religious change and the status of working-class women. *Journal of Interamerican Studies and World Affairs* 17: 4.

Freire, Gilberto. 1963. *The mansions and the shanties: The making of modern Brazil,* translated by Harriet de Onís. New York: Knopf.

Galletta, Ricardo. 1985. Pastoral popular e política partidária no Brasil, Master's thesis, Universidade Metodista de Piracicaba (SP).

————, et al. 1986. *Pastoral popular e política partidária.* São Paulo: Edições Paulinas.

Gebara, Ivone and Maria Clara Bingemer. 1988. *Maria, mãe de Deus, mãe dos pobres.* 2nd ed. Petropolis: Vozes.

Gifford, Carolyn DeSwarte. 1986. Home protection: The WCTU's conversion to woman suffrage. In Sharstanian, ed., 95–120.

Gilfeather, Katherine. 1977. The changing role of women in the Catholic Church in Chile. *Journal for the Scientific Study of Religion* 16, no. 1: 39–54.

————. 1985. Coming of age in a Latin Church. In *The church and women in the third world,* edited by C.B. John and Ellen Loro Webster, 58–73. Philadelphia: Webster Press.

Gilligan, Carol. 1982. *In a different voice.* Cambridge, Mass.: Harvard University Press.

Golden, Renny. 1991. *The hour of the poor, the hour of women: Salvadoran women speak.* New York: Crossroads/Continuum.

Goldsmit, Shulamit and Ernest Sweeney. 1988. The church and Latin American women in their struggle for equality and justice. *Thought* 63: no. 249, 176–88.

Gómez de Souza, Luiz Alberto. 1982. *Classes populares e igreja nos caminhos da história.* Petrópolis: Vozes.

Goot, Murray and Elizabeth Reid. 1984. Women: If not apolitical, then conservative. In *Women and the public sphere,* edited by Janet Siltanen and Michelle Stanworth, 122–36. New York: St. Martin's Press.

Greeley, Andrew M. 1977. *The Mary myth: On the femininity of God.* New York: Seabury Press.

Greeley, Andrew M. and Mary G. Durkin. 1984. *Angry Catholic women.* Chicago: Thomas More Press.

Gutiérrez, Gustavo. 1970. Notes for a theology of liberation. *Theological Studies* 31: 243–61.

————. 1973. *A Theology of liberation: History, politics and salvation,* translated and edited by Caridad Inda and John Eagleson. Maryknoll, N.Y.: Orbis.

————. 1979. Liberation praxis and Christian faith. In *Frontiers of theology in Latin America,* edited by R. Gibellini, 1–33. Maryknoll, N.Y.: Orbis.

Hahner, June E. 1990. *Emancipating the female sex: The struggle for women's rights in Brazil, 1850–1940.* Durham, N.C.: Duke University Press.

Heaton, Tim B. and Marie Cornwall. 1989. Religious group variation in the socioeconomic status and family behavior of women. *Journal for the Scientific Study of Religion* 28, no. 3: 283–99.

Hewitt, W. E. 1985. The structure and orientation of comunidades eclesiais de base (CEBs) in the archdiocese of São Paulo. Ph.D. diss., McMaster University (Canada).

————. 1986. Strategies for social change employed by comunidades eclesiais de base (CEBs) in the archdiocese of São

Paulo. *Journal for the Scientific Study of Religion* 25, no. 1: 16–30.

———. 1987. Maria Ferreira dos Santos. In *The human tradition in Latin America: The twentieth century,* edited by W. Beezley and J. Ewell, 245–57. Wilmington, Del.: Scholarly Resources, Inc.

———. 1989. Origins and prospects of the option for the poor in Brazilian Catholicism. *Journal for the Scientific Study of Religion* 28: 120–35.

———. 1991. *Base Christian communities and social change in Brazil.* Lincoln, Nebr.: University of Nebraska Press.

Hobsbawm, E. J. 1959. *Primitive rebels: Studies in archaic forms of social movement in the 19th and 20th centuries.* New York: W. W. Norton.

Ireland, Rowan. 1991. *Kingdoms come: Religion and politics in Brazil.* Pittsburgh: University of Pittsburgh Press.

Jaquette, Jane S. 1991. Introduction to *The women's movement in Latin America: Feminism and the transition to democracy,* 1–17. Boulder, Colo.: Westview Press.

Kaplan, Temma. 1981. Class consciousness and community in nineteenth-century Andalusia. *Political Power and Social Theory* 2: 21–57.

———. 1982. Female consciousness and collective action: The case of Barcelona, 1910–1918. In *Feminist theory: A critique of ideology,* edited by N. Keohane, M. Rosaldo, and R. Gelpi, 55–76. Chicago: University of Chicago Press.

Kaufman, Debra Renee. 1985. Women who return to orthodox Judaism: A feminist analysis. *Journal of Marriage and the Family* 47: 543–51.

Keogh, Dermot, ed. 1990. *Church and politics in Latin America.* New York: St. Martin's Press.

Klatch, Rebecca E. 1987. *Women of the new right.* Philadelphia: Temple University Press.

———. 1988a. Coalition and conflict among women of the new right. *Signs* 13, no. 4: 671–94.

———. 1988b. Of meanings and masters: Political symbolism and symbolic action. *Polity* 21: 137–54.

Krischke, Paulo and Scott Mainwaring, eds. 1986. *A igreja nas bases em tempo de transição (1974–85).* Porto Alegre: L&PM-CEDEC.

Kselman, T. 1986. Ambivalence and assumption in the concept of popular religion. In *Religion and political conflict in Latin America,* edited by Daniel Levine, 24–41. Chapel Hill: University of North Carolina Press.

Laitin, David. 1986. *Hegemony and culture: Politics and religious change among the Yoruba.* Chicago: University of Chicago Press.

————. 1988. Political culture and political preferences. *American Political Science Review* 82, no. 2 (June): 589–93.

Lamounier, Bolívar, ed. 1986. *1985: O voto em São Paulo.* São Paulo: IDESP.

Lawless, Elaine J. 1988a. *God's peculiar people: Women's voices and folk tradition in a Pentecostal Church.* Lexington, Ky.: University of Kentucky Press.

————. 1988b. *Handmaidens of the Lord: Pentecostal women preachers and traditional religion.* Philadelphia: University of Pennsylvania Press.

Leege, David C. and Michael R. Welch. 1989. Religious roots of political orientations: Variations among American Catholic parishioners. *Journal of Politics* 51, no. 1 (February): 137–62.

Lesbaupin, Ivo. 1983. As cartilhas políticas diocesanas de 1981–82. In *Igreja–Movimentos populares–Política no Brasil,* edited by Ivo Lesbaupin, 57–76. São Paulo: Edições Loyola.

Levine, Daniel H. 1978. Authority in church and society: Latin American models. *Comparative Studies in Society and History* 20, no. 4: 517–44.

————. 1980. Religion and politics, politics and religion: An introduction. In *Churches and Politics in Latin America,* edited by D. Levine, 16–40. Beverly Hills, Calif.: Sage.

————. 1981a. *Religion and politics in Latin America: The Catholic Church in Venezuela and Colombia.* Princeton: Princeton University Press.

————. 1981b. Religion, society and politics: States of the art. *Latin American Research Review* 16, no. 3: 185–209.

————. 1984. Popular organizations and the church: Thoughts from Colombia. *Journal of Interamerican Studies and World Affairs,* 26 (February): 137–42.

————. 1986a. Colombia: The institutional church and the popular. In *Religion and political conflict in Latin America,* edited by D. Levine, 187–217. Chapel Hill: University of North Carolina Press.

———. 1986b. Religion, the poor, and politics in Latin America today. In *Religion and Political Conflict in Latin America*, edited by D. Levine, 3–23. Chapel Hill: University of North Carolina Press.

———. 1989. Popular groups, popular culture and popular religion. Working paper no. 127, Helen Kellogg Institute for International Studies, University of Notre Dame.

———. 1990. The Catholic Church and politics in Latin America: Basic trends and likely futures. In *Church and politics in Latin America*, edited by Dermot Keogh, 25–48. New York: St. Martin's Press.

———. 1991. Religion. In *Latin American and Caribbean studies: A critical guide to research*, edited by Paula Covington. Westport, Conn.: Greenwood Press.

———. 1992. *Popular voices in Latin American Catholicism*. Princeton: Princeton University Press.

Levine, D. and S. Mainwaring. 1989. Religion and popular protest in Latin America: Contrasting experiences. In *Power and popular protest: Latin American social movements*, edited by Susan Eckstein, 203–40. Berkeley: University of California Press.

Levine, D. and A. Wilde. 1977. The Catholic Church, 'politics,' and violence: The Colombian case. *The Review of Politics* 39, no. 2: 220–39.

MacCormack, Carol and Marilyn Strathern, eds. 1980. *Nature, culture and gender*. New York: Cambridge University Press.

Macedo, Carmen Cinira. 1986. *Tempo de gênesis: O povo das comunidades eclesiais de base*. São Paulo: Editora Brasiliense.

Mainwaring, Scott. 1986. *The Catholic church and politics in Brazil, 1916–1985*. Stanford: Stanford University Press.

———. 1989. Grass-roots Catholic groups and politics in Brazil. In *The progressive church in Latin America*, edited by Scott Mainwaring and Alexander Wilde, 151–92. Notre Dame, Ind.: University of Notre Dame Press.

——— and Alexander Wilde. 1989. The progressive church in Latin America: An interpretation. In *The progressive church in Latin America*, edited by Scott Mainwaring and Alexander Wilde, 1–40. Notre Dame, Ind.: University of Notre Dame Press.

Mariz, Cecilia L. 1989. Religion and coping with poverty in Brazil. Ph.D. diss., Boston University.

―――. 1994. *Coping with poverty: Pentecostals and Christian base communities in Brazil*. Philadelphia: Temple University Press.

Mecham, J. L. 1966. *Church and state in Latin America*. Chapel Hill: University of North Carolina Press.

Mesters, Carlos. 1977. *Maria, A mãe de Jesus*. Petrópolis: Vozes.

Miranda, José. 1974. *Marx and the Bible: A critique of the philosophy of oppression*, translated by John Eagleson. Maryknoll, N.Y.: Orbis.

Molyneux, Maxine. 1985. Mobilization without emancipation?: Women's interests, the state, and revolution in Nicaragua. *Feminist Studies* 11, no. 2: 227–54.

Morais, Maria Lygia Quartim de. 1985. *Mulheres en movimento: O balanço da decada da mulher do ponto de vista do feminismo, das religões e da política*. São Paulo: Nobel/Conselho Estadual da Condicão Feminina.

Moser, Antônio. 1983. Aspectos morais da caminhada das CEBs no Brasil. *Revista Eclesiástica Brasileira* 43, no. 171: 504–12.

Myscofski, Carole A. 1985. Women's religious role in Brazil: A history of limitations. *Journal of Feminist Studies in Religion* 1, no. 2 (fall): 43–57.

Neitz, Mary Jo. 1993. Inequality and difference: Feminist research in the sociology of religion. In *A future for religion?* edited by William H. Swatos, 165–84. Newbury Park: Sage.

Neuhouser, Kevin. 1989. Sources of women's power and status among the urban poor in contemporary Brazil. *Signs: Journal of Women in Culture and Society* 14, no. 3: 685–702.

Nunes, Maria José Rosado. 1985. *Vida religiosa nos meios populares*. Petrópolis: Vozes.

Núñez, Emilio A. 1985. *Liberation theology*. Translated by Paul E. Sywulka. Chicago: Moody Press.

O'Connor, Sr. Francis B. 1993. *Like bread, their voices rise: Global women challenge the church*. Notre Dame, Ind.: Ave Maria.

Padilha, Solange. 1982. Características e limites das organizações de base feminina. In *Trabalhadoras do Brasil*, edited by C. Bruschini and F. Rosemberg. São Paulo: Brasiliense/Fundação Carlos Chagas.

Pateman, Carole. 1971. Political culture, political structure and political change. *British Journal of Political Science* 1: 291–305.

————. 1980. The civic culture: A philosophic critique. In *The civic culture revisited,* edited by G. Almond and S. Verba, 57–102. Boston: Little, Brown.

Peritore, N. Patrick. 1990. *Socialism, communism, and liberation theology in Brazil: An opinion survey using Q-methodology.* Latin America Series, no. 15. Athens, Ohio: Center for International Studies, Ohio University.

Perry, Nicholas and Loreto Echeverria. 1988. *Under the heel of Mary.* New York: Routledge.

Petrini, João Carlos. 1984. *CEBs: Um novo sujeito popular.* Rio de Janeiro: Paz e Terra.

Pierucci, A. F. 1984. Democracia, Igreja e voto: O envolvimento dos padres de paróquia de São Paulo nas eleições de 1982. Ph.D. diss., USP (São Paulo).

Pierucci, Antônio Flávio and Reginaldo Prandi. 1995. Religiões e voto: A eleição presidencial de 1994. *Opinião Pública* 3, no. 1: 20–44.

Porter, Judith R. and Alexa A. Albert. 1977. Subculture or assimilation? A cross-cultural analysis of religion and women's roles. *Journal for the Scientific Study of Religion* 16, no. 4: 345–59.

Reilly, C. 1986. Latin America's religious populists. In *Religion and political conflict in Latin America,* edited by D. Levine, 42–57. Chapel Hill: University of North Carolina Press.

Ricco, Ruben. 1984. Igreja e migrações internas: A Integração do migrante de baixa renda nas comunidades eclesiais de base da periferia de São Paulo. Master's thesis, IUPERJ (Rio).

Richards, Pablo, et. al. 1983. *The idols of death and the God of life: A theology,* translated by Barbara E. Campbell and Bonnie Shepard. Maryknoll, N.Y.: Orbis.

Rolim, Francisco Cartaxo. 1980a. Comunidades eclesiais de base e camadas populares. *Encontros Com a Civilização Brasileira* 22 (April): 89–114.

————. 1980b. *Religião e classes populares.* Petrópolis: Vozes.

Roozen, David A. and Jackson W. Carroll. 1979. Recent trends in church membership and participation: An introduction. In *Understanding church growth and decline,* edited by Dean R. Hoge and David A. Roozen, 21–41. Cleveland, Ohio: Pilgrim.

Ruddick, Sarah. 1982. Maternal thinking. In *Rethinking the family: Some feminist questions,* edited by B. Thorne and M. Yalom, 76–94. New York: Longman.

Sacks, Karen. 1979. *Sisters and wives: The past and future of sexual equality.* Westport, Conn.: Greenwood Press.

Saffioti, Heleieth I. B. 1979. *A mulher na sociedade de classes: Mito e realidade.* Petrópolis: Vozes.

Saiving, Valerie. 1979. The human situation: A feminine view. In *Womanspirit rising: A feminist reader in religion,* edited by Carol P. Christ and Judith Plaskow, 25–42. San Francisco: Harper and Row.

Sanders, Thomas G. 1967. Catholicism and development: The Catholic left in Brazil. In *Churches and states: The religious institution and modernization,* edited by Kalman Silvert, 81–99. New York: American Universities Field Staff.

Sanks, T. H. and B. Smith. 1977. Liberation ecclesiology: Praxis, theory, praxis. *Theological Studies* 38, no. 1: 3–38.

Sapiro, Virginia. 1983. *The political integration of women: Roles, socialization, and politics.* Urbana, Ill.: University of Illinois Press.

Scannone, Juan Carlos. 1979. Theology, popular culture, and discernment. In *Frontiers of theology in Latin America,* edited by R. Gibellini, 213–37. Maryknoll, N.Y.: Orbis.

Schmink, Marianne. 1981. Women in Brazilian *Abertura* politics. *Signs* 7, no. 1: 115–34.

Segundo, Juan Luís. 1976. *The liberation of theology.* Maryknoll, N.Y.: Orbis.

———. 1979. Capitalism versus socialism: Crux theologica. In *Frontiers of theology in Latin America,* edited by R. Gibellini, 240–59. Maryknoll, N.Y.: Orbis.

———. 1984. Two theologies of liberation. *The Month* (October): 321–27.

Schneiders, Sandra M. 1983. The effects of women's experience on their spirituality. *Spirituality Today* (summer), 100–16.

Sharistanian, Janet, ed. 1986. *Gender, ideology, and action: Historical perspectives on women's public lives.* New York: Greenwood Press.

———. 1986a. Conclusion: Historical study and the public/domestic model. In Sharistanian, ed.: 229–35.

———. 1986b. Introduction: Women's lives in the public and domestic spheres. In Sharistanian, ed.: 1–10.

Sigmund, Paul. 1990. *Liberation theology at the crossroads: Democracy or revolution?* New York: Oxford University Press.

Simões, Solange de Deus. 1985. *Deus, patria e família: As mulheres na golpe de 1964.* Petrópolis: Vozes.

Skinner, Quentin. 1969. Meaning and understanding in the history of ideas. *History and Theory* 8, no. 1: 3–53.

——. 1989. Language and political change. In *Political innovation and conceptual change,* edited by T. Ball, J. Farr, and R. Hanson, 6–23. Cambridge: Cambridge University Press.

Slater, David, ed. 1985. *New social movements and the state in Latin America.* Amsterdam: CEDLA.

Smith, B. H. 1975. Religion and social change: Classical theories and new formulations in the context of recent developments in Latin America. *Latin America Research Review* 10, no. 2: 3–34.

——. 1982. *The church and politics in Chile: Challenges to modern Catholicism.* Princeton: Princeton University Press.

Spretnak, Charlene, ed. 1982. *The politics of women's spirituality: Essays on the rise of spiritual power within the feminist movement.* Garden City, N.J.: Doubleday, Anchor.

Stevens, Evelyn P. 1973. Marianismo: The other face of machismo in Latin America. In *Female and male in Latin America,* edited by Ann Pescatello, 89–101. Pittsburgh: University of Pittsburgh Press.

Tabak, Fanny and Moema Toscano. 1982. *Mulher e política.* Rio de Janeiro: Paz e Terra.

Tannen, Deborah. 1990. *You just don't understand: Women and men in conversation.* New York: Bantam Books.

Thornton, Arland. 1985. Reciprocal influences of family and religion in a changing world. *Journal of Marriage and the Family* 47: 381–94.

Vallier, Ivan. 1970. *Catholicism, social control and modernization in Latin America.* Englewood Cliffs, N.J.: Prentice-Hall.

——. 1972a. Church 'development' in Latin America: A five country comparison. In *The Roman Catholic Church in modern Latin America,* edited by Karl M. Schmitt, 167–93. New York: Alfred A. Knopf.

——. 1972b. Radical priests and the revolution. In *Changing Latin America: New interpretations of its politics and society,* edited by D. Chalmers, 15–26. New York: Academy of Political Science.

Van den Eykel, Myrna. 1986. A comparative study of the political and social activism of new religious groups in Colombia. Ph.D. diss., George Washington University.

Van den Hoogen, Lisette. 1990. The romanization of the Brazilian Church: Women's participation in a religious association in Prados, Minas Gerais. *Sociological Analysis* 50, no. 2: 171–88.

Wald, Kenneth D., Dennis E. Owen, and Samuel S. Hill, Jr. 1988. Churches as political communities. *American Political Science Review* 82, no. 2 (June): 531–48.

Weber, Max. 1946. *From Max Weber: Essays in sociology,* translated and edited by H. H. Gerth and C. Wright Mills. New York: Oxford University Press.

———. 1958. *The Protestant ethic and the spirit of capitalism,* translated by Talcott Parsons. New York: Charles Scribner's Sons.

Welch, Michael R. and David C. Leege. 1988. Religious predictors of Catholic parishioners' sociopolitical attitudes: Devotional style, closeness to God, imagery, and agentic/communal religious identity. *Journal for the Scientific Study of Religion* 27, no. 4: 536–52.

Wiarda, Howard. 1973. Toward a framework for the study of political change in the Iberic-Latin tradition: The corporative model. *World Politics* 25 (January), 206–35.

Wildavsky, Aaron. 1987. Choosing preferences by constructing institutions: A cultural theory of preference formation. *American Political Science Review* 81, no. 1: 3–21.

Wilde, Alexander W. 1980. Ten years of change in the church: Puebla and the future. In *Churches and politics in Latin America,* edited by Daniel H. Levine, 267–79. Beverly Hills, Calif.: Sage.

PAMPHLETS AND NEWSPAPERS

Acorda, povo! 1982. Região São Miguel (June).

Aos animadores dos grupos de rua: De 1979 até 1985, recordando a caminhada dos grupos de rua no setor Itaim Paulista. 1986. Mimeo, Setor Itaim Paulista (Região São Miguel).

Calce as sandálias, é tempo de missão. 1986. Região São Miguel.

Cantos do povo de Deus. n.d. São Paulo: Ediçoes Loyola.

CEBs, povo unido, semente de uma nova sociedade. N.d. (1983?). Equipe das CEBs, Estado de São Paulo.

Estamos em assembléia. 1983. Região São Miguel.

Grita povo. Região São Miguel.

Latinamerica press.

Latin America regional reports: Brazil.

Latin America weekly reports.

Para que todos tenham vida. 1984. Região São Miguel (Campanha de Fraternidade).

Somente a ação organizada é transformadora: Preparação para a assembléia. 1983. Região São Miguel.

Tu és o Deus dos pequenos. 1986. Região São Miguel (Novena de Natal).

Um passo adiante! Cartilhas das comunidades. 1985. Região São Miguel (August).

Index